Abby,
It has been [illegible]
you + your family. I hope Libby's
life will provide you with greater
motivation to be great in Christ's
Kingdom.

In Christ,
Rom 8:18,
Ken Yates

ELISABETH

Christ's Medal of Honor Recipient

BY

KEN YATES

Grace Evangelical Society
Denton, Texas 76210

Elisabeth:
Christ's Medal of Honor Recipient

P.O. Box 1308, Denton, TX 76202
Printed in the USA

Information requests should be directed to
ges@faithalone.org, www.faithalone.org

Yates, Ken W., 1958–

Design and typesetting by Matthew Simmons
Cover photo: Elisabeth as a bridesmaid at her sister
Kathryn's wedding.

ISBN: 978-1-943399-48-2

SPECIAL ACKNOWLEDGMENTS

Elisabeth was happiest when she was part of a group. She grew up in a military family and moved many times in her life. As a result, she met many different groups of friends.

These friends were a source of great joy for her. Whether they were playing dress up, putting on a play, playing a game, having a sleepover, attending parties, taking part in homeschooling co-ops, or taking a ride in her chair, they always made her one of the group. When she was with them, that is exactly the way she felt.

As a parent, I very much appreciated all of these friends. I want to acknowledge and give thanks to them. There are many who come to mind: the Yates and Naillieux cousins and second cousins; the Tarvins; Marrs; Herberts; Ohnesorges; Andrees; Lockharts; Butlers; Hoyts; Kovaches; Uyenos; Livingstons; Cornetts; Todds; Ushers; Naethings; Gunters; and Felicity.

At times, I was tempted to think all these people were simply being nice. Upon reflection, I realized they also benefited by their association with Elisabeth. In their faces I could see it, and have no doubt that they were consciously aware of the same thing.

Another time Elisabeth was happiest was when she was in church. While I was in the army, those churches were most often military chapels. After her family was no longer part of the military, she attended two "civilian" churches. These churches also received her with open arms. There are too many individuals to acknowledge, so I will simply mention a representative from each one. Thank you, Alice and Eise. Those who were part of these churches will understand why these women were chosen as your reps.

I realize that the passage of time may have caused me to forget others who needed to be mentioned. You know who you are. To all those who made Elisabeth a part of your life, in whatever way, our family wants to say "thanks."

DEDICATION

This book is dedicated to Choop, Chaurchen, Bange, and Kit. I look forward to the day when the Captain brings the team together again (Hebrews 2:10).

It is also dedicated to Eli (Hebrews 4:14-16).

TABLE OF CONTENTS

CHAPTER ONE

Introduction

For many people, and in many cultures, the name Job is practically synonymous with suffering. He was a man who lost his many children, his wealth, and his health. His closest friends abandoned him, accusing him of things he had not done. Even his wife turned against him.

Few people in history can understand what he went through. But when we read what he endured, we can understand why he felt that a man's life is short and characterized by hardships. In the midst of his sufferings, he said:

> "Man *who is* born of woman
> Is of few days and full of trouble.
> He comes forth like a flower and fades away;
> He flees like a shadow and does not continue."
> (Job 14:1-2)

Most of us have not suffered quite as severely as Job did, but the longer we live, the more we would agree with what he had to say. In the Old Testament, he became an example for others. In him, God taught us certain things about trials. Writing more than two thousand years later, James stated that even today we can all learn lessons from the life of Job (James 5:11).

But whatever we can learn from Job when it comes to the subject of suffering, the coming and example of Jesus Christ taught us so much more. We could say that Job was like a night-light in a dark room, shining forth truth about the theme of hardships in the lives of God's people. Christ, however, is like the midday sun on a cloudless day, illuminating everything.

In the pages of the New Testament, in Christ and His teaching, we see clearly what God wants us to see about suffering. Jesus was the Teacher par excellence.

By God's grace, we can learn the lessons the Teacher taught us in His own life and observe them in the lives of others as they go through trials. When we do, it is entirely correct to say we are seeing *Him* in others.

Sometimes we are even fortunate enough to see such things in those who are close to us—people we see every day. In my life, one of those people was Elisabeth, who I called Libby. That is what this book is about.

CHAPTER TWO

One Year Later

July 14, 2021. Libby died exactly one year ago today. She was thirty-five years old. She was my daughter.

My wife Pam, our three daughters, Emily, Amy, and Kathryn, and I went to Libby's favorite restaurant for dinner in memory of her. The waitress asked if we were celebrating something, and none of us knew exactly how to answer her, so we changed the subject—partly because we didn't want her to feel bad about asking the question or uncomfortable after hearing the answer, and partly because we didn't know what to say. Were we there to celebrate her life? Were we there to feel sad about our loss and how much we missed her? But I also think we didn't tell the waitress why we were there because we wanted to remember Libby as a family in a private way.

That evening, however, I went home and began writing this book. I feel strongly that there are people who could benefit from knowing more about Libby's life.

For those reading this book, perhaps the first thing you need to know about her is that if you had met her, you wouldn't have called her by the name Libby. It was a family nickname. Her real, given, name was Elisabeth. When she was younger, everybody called her Libby. But when she was around twenty, she asked her sisters, her mom, and me if we would no longer call her that because she felt it made her sound like a little baby.

I think she may have gotten the idea from one of her favorite movies, *Anne of Green Gables.* It is a funny story of a young orphaned girl who is adopted by an elderly brother and sister who were both unmarried, childless, and looking for help on the farm they ran together.

At one point, the talkative girl asks her adopted mother if she would do her a favor and make sure she writes her name as "Ann with an e." The girl then chattered on about how "Ann" was just so plain, but Ann with an "e" (Anne) was so much more elegant.

Libby was like Ann in the movie. She took a certain amount of pride in the fact that her real name was spelled with an "s" instead of a "z". She would point out to people that the older Bibles, like the King James Version, spelled it that way. In her mind, Elisabeth was indeed an elegant name, much more so than the name Libby.

The adopted mother in the movie thought that was just silly, and told Ann that she found no reason to do what she asked. Ann was a fine and dignified name after all, and it was a practical one.

I find a little bit of comfort in that fictional encounter. In one of many parental mistakes my wife and I made during her life, we told Libby that the family would not start calling her Elisabeth. Wasn't going to happen. She was always going to be Libby to us. Her mom and I said she would always be our baby, so it didn't matter one bit that the name Libby made her sound like one.

But we did make a compromise. We told her that from now on, we would ask people outside the family to call her Elisabeth. She agreed that this was a workable solution. To our credit, from that time forward, the whole family did indeed introduce her to others as Elisabeth. But we reminded them that we would call her Libby, so that they would not get confused. She never said it, but I know that she loved that arrangement.

In keeping with that agreement, I will refer to her as "Elisabeth" as I write this book. After all, whatever readers this book may have will overwhelmingly be non-family members. Most, in fact, will probably be people who never met her. I am pretty sure Elisabeth would have smiled at this concession on my part.

To understand what will be said about Elisabeth in this book, there is something more important to know about her than what you would have called her. Elisabeth had cerebral palsy.

Cerebral palsy affects those who have it in many different ways, and has various levels of severity. It can affect the ability to speak. It can affect different parts of the body. Its impact can be mild, profound, and anything in between. The disease often results in various mental disabilities as well. Finally, a person can be afflicted with the disease at birth, or any time during his or her life.

In Elisabeth's case, she suffered injury to her brain at birth, so she had cerebral palsy her whole life. Its most obvious effect was that she lost the vast majority of the use of all four limbs. She would never walk and could only use her arms and hands in very limited ways. It was very difficult for her to sit up straight, as cerebral palsy prevented her from having enough core strength to do so.

As a result, she was dependent upon others her whole life. She could not care for herself in any way. If somebody prepared certain finger foods, she could eat them (with great difficulty). But she could not dress herself, clean herself, go to the bathroom, get in bed, or get up on her own. She never took a step, but had to use a wheelchair her whole life. In certain circumstances she could use an electric wheelchair, but most of the time she utilized a manual one that was pushed by a family member or friend.

Fortunately, cerebral palsy did not affect her voice. She could talk clearly and, like *Anne of Green Gables,* loved to do so. She would talk about the movies she had seen, or the books she had listened to on tape. Stories in the Bible and even politics were some of her favorite topics to discuss with others. It was easy to carry on a conversation with her.

In fact, it was so easy that when doing so you sometimes forgot that cerebral palsy had left her with certain learning disabilities as well. Elisabeth could only read slowly and with great difficulty. Weakness in her eyes contributed to that situation. Things others take for granted, such as figuring out the price of something, or how much change you would get back from a twenty-dollar bill if an item cost ten dollars, were beyond her ability to figure out. She could not carry out the simplest of math problems. The same could be said about things like geography. She could tell you what state she was in, but would not be able to show you on a map where that state was located.

An interesting aspect of her physical and mental disabilities was her sense of humor and her ability to negotiate certain social situations. She could not always understand sarcasm and would often assume people were serious when they were only joking. On many such occasions her sisters, mom, and I reminded her that she had no sense of humor and pointed out that the person she was talking to was not being serious.

In the same light, Elisabeth would not always know if it was appropriate to say certain things. She would never want to hurt somebody's feelings by saying the wrong thing, and it would have been devastating to her if she did so. I will never know how often that happened, but I know there were many times she chose not to say something just to make sure she didn't say the wrong thing and hurt somebody else.

In these social situations she also didn't want to appear, in her words, "dumb." She realized she didn't always understand the nuance of what was going on and would remain silent so as not to let others figure out that "secret" of hers. If there was an inside joke that she didn't understand, she would prefer that others thought she was in on it as well.

Simply put, my daughter Elisabeth lived a life full of difficulties. Just how hard certain things were for her, those of us without cerebral palsy simply cannot know. I came to realize that the disease caused her to experience more pain and discomfort than our family was even aware of. She simply accepted such things as part of her life.

On the other hand, there were sad parts of her life that all who knew her could grasp. She would never go on a first date or marry. Even though she said she would have loved to have become a mother, that would never become a reality for her. The college experience would be out of her reach, as would holding a job and eventually becoming an independent adult, striking out in the world on her own. I am not completely sure how she processed her situation as she saw her sisters, other relatives, and friends experience all these things. I never heard her express resentment or jealousy.

The fact of the matter was that she knew she would always depend on her family to care for her. While most might look at a situation like that and think how hard that was on the family, it is easy to overlook how hard it was for a person like Elisabeth. It is not an exaggeration to say it was harder for her, even in this area.

For a number of years, Elisabeth attended a summer camp in Missouri called Camp Barnabas, which hosts hundreds of children with a vast range of physical and mental disabilities. The adult cabin leaders supervise ten to twelve campers each, and each camper is also assigned at least one young helper, a high school or college student, to assist with all his or her needs. The campers and their aides participate in all kinds of activities together. The goal of the camp is to provide a summer camp experience where the campers are not excluded from anything they offer, from water slides to canoeing to archery. Elisabeth loved going to the camp because so often in her life her disease prevented her from doing what those around her were doing. (As a side note, I cannot express how much my family and I are grateful to Camp Barnabas.)

The campers love to stay awake on their bunks and talk before they go to sleep each night. This is an opportunity for teenagers who understand each other's struggles to talk about them together. We can perhaps imagine how much more open they are with each other than with those who don't understand.

One year, Elisabeth's cabin "mom" told me that as she listened to the kids converse, they had something in common: they all said they wished they weren't such a burden to those who loved them. In other words, these kids were laden down with another difficulty that they often didn't want to share even with those closest to them.

It is just heartbreaking to realize that in addition to the obvious difficulties Elisabeth faced, there were others that were not as obvious. Through the years, for example, I realized that there were so many things we take for granted that she couldn't do. If she was in an uncomfortable position in her bed at night, she couldn't adjust her body to a more comfortable one. She also told me on a number of occasions that she wished people who didn't know her would talk directly to her when they met her, rather than talking to me, or her mom, or her sisters about her, even though she was right there! She would say, "They see my wheelchair and assume I cannot talk. I think sometimes, especially little kids are afraid of me." I sometimes wonder how many things like this escaped my notice.

I say all of these things just so that you, the reader, can get a picture of what Elisabeth's life was like—what *she* was like. Each person is complex, and she was no different in that regard. However, she lived in our home for thirty-five years, and most people have not had a person with her kind of physical and mental circumstances live with them for such an extended period of time. Naturally, it is difficult for most people to understand what that involves. But I cannot share the lessons I learned from Elisabeth without first providing some kind of mental picture of these things. She was a living illustration of incredible truths, and our family was fortunate enough to have her under our roof for all those years. We learned so much from that experience.

But everyone can benefit from her example. And that is the purpose of this book. Most of us cannot relate to the circumstances of Elisabeth's life. But to some degree, we all have difficulties. We will experience the loss of loved ones. We will get sick. If we live long enough, almost all of us will need to rely on others. We might lose our livelihoods or businesses. The list goes on and on. Some will have even more difficulties than Elisabeth did. I am convinced that the things I learned from watching her can help all of us as we go through whatever trials we face both now and in the future.

In talking about her, however, I want the reader to know I am not as blind as some might conclude. As I describe certain events in her life, one might be tempted to assume I am exaggerating. I am, after all, a biased father. Dads are often accused of thinking their little girls are perfect and can do no wrong. It would be easy to read the words written here and conclude that I have fallen into that trap when it comes to what I have to say about Elisabeth.

I will admit that Elisabeth is my hero. My dad was a career solider, who was in the military the whole time I was growing up. I spent almost thirty years in the military myself. As a result, I have met many heroes, and I know what they look like—men and women who are braver and better people than I am.

The United States Congress awards the Medal of Honor to the bravest of the brave in the military—it is the highest honor our nation can give a soldier. It is extremely rare—there are only about one hundred recipients living today—and their stories of bravery and sacrifice are truly awe-inspiring. Most who have received the medal did so at the cost of their own lives in battle, often by saving the lives of others. The honor is so great, it is improper to speak of a Medal of Honor "winner." They are called "recipients" because what they did is so heroic, they are given this honor by a grateful nation as recognition from the country they served.

When I was in the military, I had the privilege of working with two Medal of Honor recipients, and I met a few others after I retired. Of all the soldiers I have had the privilege of knowing, they surely stood apart.

But Elisabeth was the greatest hero I ever met. Oh, I am sure there are others who were and are greater, but I haven't been given the honor of living with them for over three decades. I was able to see Elisabeth's life up close and personal.

Let me assure you, though, that I know Elisabeth was not perfect. Like all of us, she was a sinner. The Apostle Paul perhaps said it best when he wrote in Romans 3:10, "There is none righteous, not even one." A few verses later, he says, "For all have sinned and fall short of the glory of God" (Romans 3:23). These words were true of her, just as they are for all of us. The fact that she was my daughter and that she was clearly a better person than I am—a spiritual hero, if you will—does not change what Paul reveals about all of us.

But the lessons from her life are not found in the universal truth that we all sin. They are found someplace else. More accurately, they are found in *Someone* else. It may sound strange to say about a book whose title is *Elisabeth,* but when everything has been said, this book is not about my daughter at all.

Jesus Christ is the subject of this book. It is about what *He* did in Elisabeth's life. The fact that she was a sinner only magnifies what He did. It magnifies His power and grace. All of her physical difficulties just add to the absolute wonder of who He is and what He has done for her. I was simply a witness to these things, and I am just sharing what I saw in the hope that it can be of help to others. The bottom line is that what Christ did for her, He can do for any of us.

First Thing's First

To understand what Jesus did *in* Elisabeth, it is best to start at the best thing He did *for* her. Elisabeth, even from a young age, loved to hear stories from the New Testament about Jesus. She was well aware of a promise He had made, a promise that is good news for all of us. He repeated this promise on many occasions, to many different people.

To a religious man, Christ said, "For God so loved the world that He gave His only Son." Jesus is the Son of God that the Father gave to the world. The Son would die on a cross to pay for the sins of the whole world. As a result, Jesus made a promise: "All who believe in Him will not perish but have everlasting life" (John 3:16).

He made the same promise to a sexually immoral woman as they talked by a well. If she only believed that He had the gift of eternal life and the ability to give it to her, she too would receive it and possess it forever (John 4:10-14).

To a large group of people listening to Him, Jesus promised the same thing. If they would believe in Him for it, they would have eternal life (John 5:24). To another group, He guaranteed that "the one who believes in Him has eternal life" (John 6:47).

I think Elisabeth's favorite account in Christ's life was the conversation He had with a friend of His named Martha. Martha's brother, Lazarus, had died four days earlier, and Jesus and Martha were standing at his tomb. Jesus promised this friend of His:

> "I am the resurrection and the life. He who believes in Me, though he were dead, yet shall he live. And he who believes in Me shall never die" (John 11:25-26).

Elisabeth understood exactly what Jesus was saying. He was saying that anybody, *including her*, who believed in Him for eternal life would receive it from Him.

But she also knew He spoke of a resurrection. If she believed in Him for eternal life, He also promised that one day her body would rise from the dead. He was promising that her body, which was ravaged by cerebral palsy, was only temporary. An eternity awaited her—an eternity in which she would live in a different kind of body altogether. A body that was not racked by pain and discomfort. A body that would not require her to be dependent upon others for her every need.

Because of what the Lord had done for her and what He had promised her, Elisabeth believed the Apostle Paul's description of our present bodies, as well as what the bodies of believers in Jesus Christ will be like in eternity:

> "It (our present body) is sown a perishable body (when it goes into the grave), it is raised an imperishable body. It is sown in dishonor, it is raised in glory. It is sown in weakness, it is raised in power" (1 Corinthians 15:42-43).

Can you imagine what Elisabeth thought when she believed these words? She knew all too well about a physical body that was "perishable" and wasting away. She knew that her earthly body would only garner pity, not honor. That pity would cause people to avoid eye contact and conversation with her, or perhaps they didn't talk to her because they thought she was "dumb." She certainly knew about a body that was full of "weakness," one that would not even allow her to take care of everyday functions.

But here was the Son of God Himself, telling her that He loved her. He was promising her an eternal existence with Him. And that existence would be one in which she would have an "imperishable" body that was full of "glory" and "power." In that body, the limitations of cerebral palsy would be a thing of the past.

Many people today hear such promises and are skeptical for various reasons, including self-sufficiency. If we are well educated, healthy, strong, or perhaps rich, it is often more difficult to think about eternity. Why should we look forward to eternity in the kingdom of God and a new body when the present age and our current body are just fine?

Such self-sufficiency might also lead one to simply not believe such an offer. After all, would Christ really offer a gift that great for free? Surely, a person must do something for it. As the saying goes, "There is no such thing as a free lunch." It stands to reason that eternal life, the greatest gift of all, cannot be free.

Many even question whether there will be any kind of existence after this life. If there is, the religions of the world are full of people who are convinced that they must do good works if they are going to be part of the eternal kingdom of God.

The Bible tells us that the Holy Spirit plays an indispensable role when a person comes to faith in Christ for eternal life. The Spirit convinces the unbeliever of the truth of who Jesus is and the gift He has to give (John 16:7-11). Nobody can come to faith without this work of the Spirit as He reveals this truth—shines a light on this truth— to all who hear the message (John 6:44; 2 Corinthians 4:4).

But those who hear may not believe what the Spirit reveals to them. They may be unwilling to believe it (John 5:40). Again, a common reason for this is human pride or self-sufficiency. But here was the first great work of God that I saw Him do in Elisabeth: she did not have any such obstacle. Feelings of self-sufficiency were not a problem for her because she was totally dependent upon others. She knew she was "weak." When the Spirit of God revealed to her that the greatest Man who ever lived said that she would live with Him forever and that He would give her a glorious body in the resurrection, she simply believed what she heard. It was completely free. As horrible as cerebral palsy was in her life, God used it to help prepare her to receive the greatest gift in the universe.

Many would describe this kind of faith as childlike, and that is exactly what it was. While some would scoff at the simplicity of such a belief, Jesus said that only that kind of faith would result in eternal life. In a well-known encounter where some children approached Jesus, the adults around Him tried to push the kids away. But He took the children in His arms, blessed them, and reminded those around

Him that childlike faith is required for entrance into the kingdom of God (Mark 10:15).

A child does not come to his parent expecting to work for acceptance, or thinking he has to work to become the parent's child. The child is dependent upon the parent and believes what he says.

When the Lord said that by faith alone Elisabeth would receive eternal life from Him and be His child forever, she never doubted. This is the very definition of a childlike faith.

Her easy willingness to believe was such that I don't even know when it happened. She was homeschooled by her mom for much of her life, and my educated guess is that she first understood and believed in Jesus at home when my wife spoke to her about Him. Whenever it was, she expressed the assurance that she would live with the Lord forever from a young age. Another one of the wonderful works of the Spirit in her life was that she maintained that childlike faith her whole life.

Because she would have cerebral palsy for thirty-five years, you could say she was like a child all those years, living her life in dependence upon others. I suppose that, from a human perspective, it also helped her to simply rely upon the Lord to do what He had promised her.

This is one of the areas where the reader might accuse a dad of exaggerating. But I assure you I am not. She *never* wavered in her faith when it came to knowing where she would spend eternity. She always knew she would be with the Lord. I am grateful for whatever role her difficulties played in that regard.

But What About...?

Elisabeth, then, knew that she was a child of God through faith in Christ. She knew that would always be the case. But in one sense, that knowledge could possibly cause a problem for her. I always wondered what she thought when she heard stories of the Lord healing people in the New Testament. She knew He had the power to do so. She believed all the stories about how He had caused the blind to see, the deaf to hear, and people who could not walk, like herself, to walk. What did she think when she heard those wonderful miraculous accounts?

She knew she was His child. She knew He could heal her, and she knew He loved her. She believed He had demonstrated that love by dying on a cross for her. However, she never asked why He didn't do for her what He had done for so many others in the stories she heard.

In Mark 2:1-12, a man who cannot walk is lowered by his friends on a cot through a roof to be placed in front of Jesus. These friends want Jesus to cure their friend, but there is a large crowd in the house listening to Christ speak, and they cannot get close to Him. That is why they dug up the roof and lowered their friend through the hole. The Lord, of course, sees the crippled man and tells him to pick up the cot he was lying on and go home. He does so, to the amazement of all who were there.

Elisabeth and I had an ongoing joke. I would ask her, "When we go to be with the Lord, would it be alright if I brought your wheelchair along?" She would give a short laugh and say, "On that day I will never want to see that chair again." She appreciated what it did for her, but when she no longer needed it, she wanted to leave it far behind.

So, what did Elisabeth think when she heard the story about the man in Mark 2? Did she wonder what it would have been like for her to get up from her chair and walk home in front of a crowd? The idea of leaving that chair behind and walking away would have been a thrilling one for her.

If I were in her situation, I am almost positive I would have been bitter sometimes about being afflicted with a disease that prevented me from walking. That bitterness would become stronger when I heard about this guy in Mark 2 and his friends. If Jesus did what He did for that young man, what about me?

It may sound strange, but Elisabeth and I never had that conversation. First of all, I didn't want to ask her about it because I was afraid she would do what I thought I would do if I were in her shoes. I didn't want her to think about it and become angry or bitter at God. I couldn't see any value in that.

But another reason, which is beyond my understanding, is that she did not have those questions. She never expressed bitterness or anger toward God for not healing her, even when she went through her trials. I can only conclude that this was another supernatural miracle I had the privilege of witnessing. Christ, living through her in His Spirit, produced in her a heart that submitted to His will for her. As a result, she simply accepted that Christ knew what He was doing. If the Lord wanted to heal the man in Mark 2, but not her, that was OK.

On numerous occasions, however, we did talk about a cure for cerebral palsy. When Elisabeth talked about such things, she was referring to a medical cure by the physicians of this world. Though she understood perfectly well that cerebral palsy would not exist in the world to come, she would mention in passing how great it would be if doctors would find such a cure in the present age. She had spent a lot of time with doctors who had helped her in many different ways, and I think she always had a glimmer of hope that they would be able to find a way for her to walk in this life.

I never pushed this thinking too hard. Maybe I was a bad parent, but I didn't want her to get her hopes up. What were the odds that they would discover such a cure? I had witnessed the impact cerebral palsy could have, and I didn't have a lot of hope that doctors could do something about it. Plus, as Elisabeth got older, the disease had impacted so much of her body. I am not a doctor, but I knew that her bones had not formed properly, and her ligaments had shrunk. Even if her brain could be fixed to initiate the motion of walking, her bones could not bear her weight, and her ligaments could not function properly. Even if the medical world could somehow figure out how to get her brain to communicate with all four of her limbs, it wouldn't have mattered in her case.

In these conversations, I would often say something like,

> "Who knows? Medical advancements have come so far. But it really doesn't matter, because one day you are going to see the One who will heal you. He has promised that you will see Him face to face. On that day you will no longer have cerebral palsy. It is a certainty that your cure is coming."

Invariably, the conversation would end with one of us saying, "You know, it could be today."

Elisabeth's Mark 2

That day arrived on July 14, 2020. Elisabeth's mom, two of her sisters, and I were with her at home. None of us had any idea what would happen on that day. One second, she was talking to us. The next second she was gone.

Many readers have experienced a similar loss in their lives. You understand when I say that it was absolutely crushing. Your life changes and you will never be the same. We all miss her, and even today we walk by her room and momentarily forget she is not there.

But this profound sadness is accompanied by such joy. In her room that day, a miracle took place. We couldn't see it with our eyes, but we have the words of the Son of God Himself that it occurred. Elisabeth "walked" into His presence. The body that was left in the room with us was twisted from the effects of cerebral palsy, and covered by many surgical scars. But Elisabeth was not there.

The Apostle Paul says that to be absent from the body (that is, when the believer dies) is to be present with the Lord (2 Corinthians 5:8). Elisabeth's soul is with her King. She now only waits for the time when He will raise her body into one full of power and glory. Her soul will be united with that body forever. The One who cannot lie has promised her that.

All believers will have a wonderful experience when they die and go to be with the Lord, but surely there is an even deeper kind of joy that somebody like Elisabeth has. I often think of what it must have been like for her that day—the day she had been waiting for all her life. She slept the previous night with her usual aches and pains, and waited for her mom or sisters to get her up, feed her, and clean her, not realizing that *He* was about to change everything for her. I wish I could have seen her face when she realized what had happened to her.

As her dad, I could stop right here. This is a story about what Jesus Christ did for my daughter. He gave her eternal life. On July 14,

2020, He did what no doctor on earth could do for her when He cured her of her cerebral palsy. Such is the greatness of Elisabeth's Savior. What more could be said?

But He is so great, there is much more to tell. In Elisabeth's life I was able to see some of His greatness. In the life to come I will see even more. Every believing reader of this book will as well.

CHAPTER THREE

Who Sinned, Lord?

There is a well-known incident in the life of Jesus that deals with an adult man who was born blind. In first-century Israel, he must have been a pitiful sight. Since there were no social programs in that society, he had been relegated to a life of begging simply to survive.

His parents, who play a role in the story, would not have foreseen this kind of life when they found out they were pregnant many years earlier. They would have been particularly happy when they had a boy. Sons were especially valued, and he would have been a kind of retirement program for them. In a society without a stock market, he was going to be their 401(k). In their old age they could have expected him to care for them.

But things did not turn out as they had expected. Instead, their son had become a financial burden to them.

No doubt, those who knew this family saw them as an unfortunate one. But there was another burden this family had to bear: the religious leaders in their society taught that this family's situation was the result of some rebellion against God by the parents. God blessed those who obeyed Him with health and wealth, they thought, and punished those who didn't with poverty and sickness. This family lived with the social stigma that their situation was the result of some kind of sin.

Since such views were part of the culture, we can assume that at least on some occasions the parents themselves thought they had brought this suffering upon their son. Some neighbors probably reminded them of this way of thinking. Even if such sentiments were not verbally expressed, the blind man and his parents surely thought they were being harshly judged in the eyes of their fellow Jews.

It did not help that the Bible in that community was thought to support such a judgment. God had given the nation laws by which to live, summarized in what would later be called the Ten Commandments. When God gave them, He told the people that if any of them rebelled against Him, the results of that sin would be felt by the children and grandchildren of the guilty person (Exodus 20:5). Is that what they were experiencing?

Jesus' twelve disciples gave voice to this way of thinking when they saw the blind man begging on the side of road. Bluntly, they asked Christ, "Who sinned, Lord, this man or his parents, that he should be born blind?" (John 9:2). It is likely the man heard these men ask this question. It was a question and sentiment he had heard many times before.

Most people today recognize that this question is a totally inadequate explanation for why there is suffering in the world. Sure, people make poor decisions with consequences that can be devastating for themselves and others. For example, a drunk driver can end up killing or injuring others, even children, bringing great pain to himself and his family. His actions could even affect his grandchildren.

But many times, perhaps even most of the time, we can't attribute people's difficulties to a bad decision or sin. And neither can they. In addition, we all know very immoral people who are rich and healthy, and many others who are better people than ourselves who are poor and have been struck with various illnesses.

Still, when we see suffering, the inadequate opinion of the disciples—or at least some variation of it—can creep into our hearts. If we see others go through extreme difficulties, we might at least entertain the idea that God is displeased with something they did—if not a sin, perhaps an unwise decision of some kind. Suffering people tend to occasionally think the same thing about themselves. They wonder if God is punishing them, even when they have no idea what they might have done wrong.

Our family experienced that.

I mentioned in the previous chapter that Elisabeth's condition existed since birth. She and the blind man had that in common. Because she was born too early, her lungs were underdeveloped, so she was not able to breathe on her own. This lack of oxygen caused the injury to her brain that resulted in cerebral palsy.

What I did not mention is that Elisabeth was a twin. Her twin's name is Amy. Pam's pregnancy was high risk. The doctors think that because of an abnormality in Elisabeth's intestines during the pregnancy, my wife produced too much amniotic fluid. While doctors were treating this problem, the fluid became infected and the twins had to be born via an emergency C-section.

Pam and I were in our mid-twenties. As a young couple, we simply wanted our girls to live. Being so young, we did not have a firm grasp on what their premature birth could mean for all of us. In fact, we didn't dwell on it. I think we just told ourselves that if they could only live, we could cross whatever bridge we had to at a later time.

Pam and I would come to a lot of bridges to cross. Elisabeth remained in intensive care for two months, and Amy for three. Both girls experienced brain bleeds immediately after birth. Holes developed in the lungs of both of them. Elisabeth underwent intestinal surgery a few days after birth. Amy experienced the buildup of fluid on her brain that caused her head to swell. While in the hospital, Amy had to have one of her lungs removed.

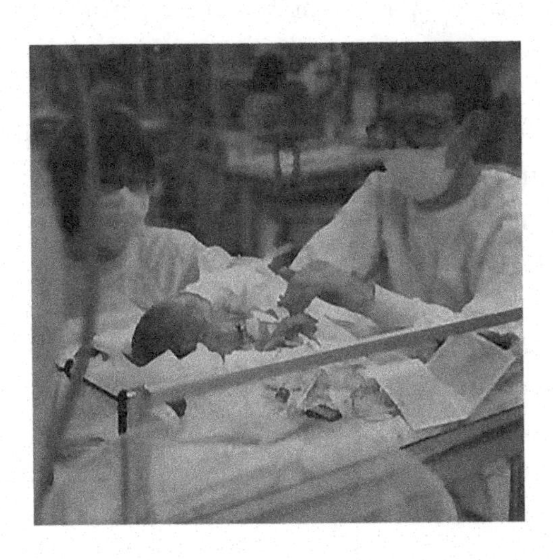

Elisabeth with her mom and dad, the day after she was born.

Both girls came home from the hospital on breathing and heart monitors. At a young age, they had surgery to repair weaknesses in their eyes. They would later have orthopedic operations to adjust the ligaments in their legs. They both would need regular physical and occupational therapy, especially in their younger years.

As they grew, Elisabeth and Amy continued to have physical challenges. Both were diagnosed with cerebral palsy. Amy eventually learned to walk, but one side of her body was weaker and smaller than the other, causing balance issues. Because of the fluid buildup in her brain, she had a shunt surgically inserted to release the pressure and several more surgeries to replace it at various times. When she was ten, she had her first noticeable seizure and was diagnosed with epilepsy.

Amy's mental abilities were different from Elisabeth's. She could read aloud much more proficiently, but could not remember what she read. She suffered noticeable short-term memory loss but could remember details, such as dates and names involved in events that happened years before. Strangely, she did not have her sister's ability to discuss politics, a movie she had seen, or a book she had read. Amy has these limitations today, and our family is blessed that she still lives with us.

Elisabeth also had reproductive problems that required her to have a hysterectomy when she was sixteen. To help alleviate her pain associated with cerebral palsy, she had a mechanical pump surgically placed in her abdomen to emit medicine into her spine. This pump had to be replaced at certain intervals.

When I think about the man born blind and his parents, I have no way of knowing what kind of medical care they would have tried, or even if any was available for them. But I imagine that, like Pam and me, the parents learned what it was like to have a blind son as they went along. There were new "discoveries" every day. I picture the mother shouldering the majority of the pressure of caring for the boy at home, as her husband went to work to support the family. That was certainly the case with our family as Pam was the one who did the majority of doctor appointments, overnight hospital stays, and teaching of the girls, as well as the other household responsibilities.

In addition, the twins had an older sister, Emily, who needed her parents' care as well.

My guess is that we shared another thing in common with the parents of the man born blind. As a young couple we did not have much money. Fortunately, my job as a security guard provided good health insurance, but certain aspects of care for the twins were not covered, and what money we did have was soon depleted by those expenses. For the first few years after the birth of the twins, we would find ourselves *way* below the poverty line. Eventually, our medical insurance reached the maximum it would pay and we were forced to rely on the government for their costs, which required me to quit working. We could only barely make ends meet with the help of government assistance in various forms.

As Christians, how were we to interpret what was happening to us and the twins? The parents of the man born blind heard the whispers from their neighbors. They knew what some of the religious leaders in the local synagogue were saying about their circumstances. They were even confronted by people who pointed out that obviously, some sin somewhere in their family had brought these things upon them. Even the disciples of the Lord thought that was the case. They asked their question about him even though they were traveling with the greatest Bible teacher who ever lived. They certainly assumed the Bible supported what they thought about this man.

I must admit I do not understand the thinking that would suggest the man was born blind because *he* had sinned. How could he have sinned before he was born? But this was a possibility in the minds of the disciples when they asked Jesus what had happened to him.

In our case, that possibility never even entered my mind. You simply cannot look at premature twins with tubes running in and out of their bodies in an intensive care room and conclude that their sufferings are the result of something they had done. They didn't even have a consciousness of what was happening to them in the present.

But the issue of *my* sin was a different story. It is probably human nature, but on rare occasions I would entertain the possibility that I had done something to bring this about.

Others were willing to consider that as well. I can tell the reader that even though it came from a small minority of people we knew, there were some Christian friends of ours who told Pam and me that we had clearly sinned and we needed to confess that sin.

Upon reflection, however, that premise did not make any sense. If *I* developed cerebral palsy, or epilepsy, I would be willing to discuss the possibility that I had done something to bring that upon myself. I could examine my life and sort through the many things I had done that displeased God to try and determine the cause. But the notion that those two girls were suffering because God was disciplining me for something I had done, was against everything I understood about Jesus Christ. It is not possible to read the New Testament, and the accounts of Christ, and conclude He would do this to these children to bring me to confess some sin that I was unaware of. When Jesus interacted with children it was with love and tenderness.

When parents brought their children to Jesus, the disciples shooed them away. The disciples thought the little ones were a nuisance. But Jesus rebuked the disciples, telling them to let the children come to Him. He took them in His arms, hugging and blessing them (Mark 10:13-16).

In another incident, one of the most tender scenes in all of the New Testament, Jesus entered the room of a little girl who had died. He took her by the hand, addressed her as "little girl," and raised her from the dead (Mark 5:41-43). Such episodes in the life of Christ demonstrate that He would not punish my little girls for some sin that I had done.

But there was another possibility that I was more open to consider: maybe Pam or I had done something that, while not sinful, caused the girls to have these problems. Maybe we should have picked a different doctor or hospital, used different prenatal vitamins, or one of a thousand other things. Maybe the disciples' question could be reworded. "Lord, what bad decision or irresponsible action by the father caused these children to be so sick?"

I suppose every person who experiences difficulties or great loss goes through this process to some degree. They think that if they had done things differently, they wouldn't be going through what they are

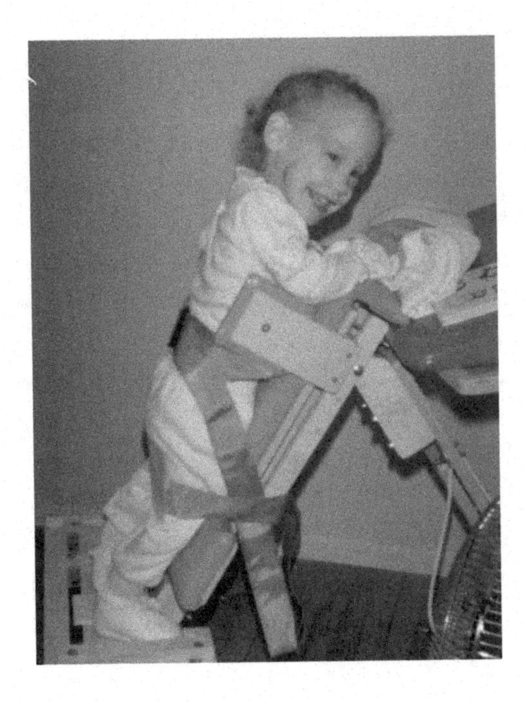

Elisabeth, at three years of age, in one of her physical therapy sessions

going through. They blame themselves and beat themselves up over it. Such thinking can even drive a person insane or ruin their health.

In this area, fortunately, I received help from an elderly Christian man. Speaking on the topic of suffering, he commented that we must "give room for the sovereignty of God." His point was that God is in control of all things. If Pam should have taken another vitamin for the good of the girls, or if we should have gone to another doctor for better care, the Lord could have compensated for those decisions. He is, after all, the Author of life and the Creator of all things. If He desired for my girls to be healthy, my ignorance in whatever area would not override that. Thousands of babies were born healthy in the same hospital where the twins were born, following the same prenatal care, using the same doctor. It wasn't our fault.

In many instances, it is simply God's will that His people go through hard times. We may not understand all the reasons why God chose us for these ordeals, but there are two things we know with absolute certainty.

The first is that God loves us. He loves Elisabeth (yes, still!) and Amy. The Bible is crystal clear on this point. God loves the world (John

3:16). God is love (1 John 4:8). Jesus loved Elisabeth to such a degree that He died on a cross so that she could receive eternal life from Him as a free gift (Romans 5:8; 1 John 4:10). It was difficult to see her go through what she did, and to lose her at such a young age, but the fact that she was loved by her Savior was never in doubt.

The second thing is perhaps much harder for us to believe, but just as clear in the Bible: *God sends sufferings for the good of His children.*

We might recoil at such an idea when we first encounter these sufferings. How could the sufferings and early death of Elisabeth be good for her? Certainly, the majority of the world would look at her as an object of pity. What possible good could come from what she went through?

I already mentioned one such good thing. Elisabeth's difficulties made it much easier for her to have a childlike faith. Such a faith pleases the Lord. But her difficulties also produced other good things.

Elisabeth and the Man Born Blind

I love the parallels of Elisabeth's life with the man born blind in John 9. They both suffered from their illness since birth. We can guess that the man, when he was healed, was around the same age as Elisabeth when she died since the man's parents were still alive. In other words, both Elisabeth and the blind man endured their difficulties for roughly the same period of time. They both had to deal with the issue of whether a sin on their part, or more likely, a sin on the part of their parents, had somehow brought all this upon them. They both understood that at least some people around them saw them in that light and concluded that they deserved what they were going through.

But Jesus' words to the blind man are like the rays of the sun coming into a dark room when the curtains are opened. They are for me, they were for Elisabeth, and they should be for every believer who is experiencing suffering. When the disciples asked who had caused this man to live in such a way—who had sinned—the Lord had an answer they did not expect: nobody. Instead, the man was born blind so "that the works of God should be revealed in him" (John 9:3).

How profound are these words! This man was born blind so that God could work in him. God was going to show others what He could do through this man. This man was going to be a walking advertisement of the power of God.

Exactly how did God do that? The most obvious way was when Jesus healed this man of his blindness. The people in Jerusalem had a clear example of the power of God at work in Christ. The man's neighbors soon learned what had happened to him (John 9:9-12). Then, he was called before the Pharisees, the religious leaders at the synagogue.

Even though they saw the power of God in what had happened, these Pharisees did not believe that Jesus was the Christ who would give eternal life to them by simply believing in Him for it. It is not surprising, then, that they also had serious reservations about what the man said to them about the One who had healed him.

These educated religious leaders brought the man before them to ask him how he had gained his sight. The man told them Jesus had healed him. They told the man that Jesus was a sinner and that God had not sent Him. In boldness, the man told them that no sinner could do what Jesus had done. After all, nobody had ever opened the eyes of a man born blind. In response, the Pharisees reminded the man that he had been blind all those years because of his sin (John 9:34).

As we have already seen, that was not the first time this man had heard that accusation. It would have been easy for this man to simply accept this verdict by such powerful and supposedly holy men and remain silent. But he was not timid in proclaiming what God had done for him through Christ. In anger, these religious leaders kicked the man out of the synagogue.

To be kicked out of the synagogue in that culture had many negative consequences. Even though he had been miraculously healed and could now see, the actions of these religious leaders ensured he would remain a social outcast. Those who were not allowed to be a part of the synagogue fell into that category.

Afterwards, Jesus approached the man and informed him that He was the Christ, and the man believed in Him. Not only did this man receive his physical sight on that day, but his spiritual eyes were opened to the truth that Jesus was the Christ, and he received eternal life when he believed.

What a privileged position this man found himself in. Even though he was poor, uneducated, and socially ostracized, he had the honor of being a witness of the King of kings. He became a clear example of what God could do. He was able to stand up in the synagogue and proclaim these truths. He showed the religious leaders *their* blindness. The leaders were blind to who Jesus was, the gift He had to give, and His power. This man became an object lesson for everyone in his nation. God had used him to show that Jesus was their long-awaited Christ. In gaining spiritual sight he became an example for all to follow.

But a reader may ask an important question here. Was it worth it? Was being the vessel through which Christ would show His power worth thirty-five years of blindness? Was having the privilege of boldly proclaiming what Christ had done for him and pointing out the blindness of others and their need for spiritual sight worth all the sufferings he had gone through?

How would this man have responded to these questions? After he had believed in Jesus as the Christ and received eternal life from Him, could he even say he was *glad* he had been born blind? As strange as it may seem to some, the answer must be yes. Such difficulties had provided him an opportunity to show the works of God, to be a bold witness for the Lord, and God had even used his sufferings to help bring him to faith and to receive eternal life. He had the privilege of being a messenger to the whole nation. He went from an object of pity, to a man whom all could emulate.

In comparing him to the religious leaders of the day, we can see how his blindness had given him an advantage. The leaders were not willing to believe in Jesus because it would mean the end of their authority. If Jesus was the Christ, they would have to submit to *His* authority. These men enjoyed a favored status among the people, a status they would lose when the Christ came. The blind man did not have such obstacles to believing in Jesus. His poverty meant he had little to give up by believing in Him. He had no authority to lose. The power of God demonstrated in his healing by Jesus was more than enough for him to believe that Jesus was the Christ.

The miraculous change that Jesus brought to this man naturally led him to publicly proclaim what had happened to him. The threat of being kicked out of the synagogue and losing status would have meant a great deal to most citizens of Jerusalem, especially these religious leaders. Even the blind man's parents were afraid to speak up about what had happened to their son because they were afraid of what the Jewish authorities would do to them (John 9:22). But such threats meant nothing to this man. He had already spent his whole life as a social outcast, so he had no fear in telling the nation what Jesus had done for him. The threats of men in power meant very little to him. When the leaders said Jesus was a sinner, this man publicly pointed out the obvious fact that Jesus had been sent from God. This healed man was a walking billboard that reminded all who saw him that nobody had ever opened the eyes of somebody born blind. Jesus was clearly the Christ.

In his earthly life, this man's healing provided a clear demonstration of the power of God. But an even greater question is this: is it possible that this man will also show the power of God in the world to come? To gain the opportunity to honor God by speaking the truth in front of the religious leaders of the day, he had to experience years of suffering. Could it be that in Christ's kingdom, he will be given some type of reward for what he endured? In other words, will God recompense this man for the price he paid in order to glorify His Son?

We do not have to guess. The New Testament says that those believers who remain faithful to the Lord in the midst of difficulties will be greatly rewarded for it for all eternity. In the pages that follow, we will look at what the New Testament says of these things.

Here it only needs to be said that the rewards God will give to such believers are more than we can imagine. God is not cheap. When He pays His servants for what they do, they will be greatly compensated. Whatever price they had to pay to honor Him, will be more than worth it.

Of course, we do not know with absolute certainty if this man continued to boldly proclaim what Jesus had done for him and that He had come from God. But he got off to a very good start! He stood up to the powerful men who opposed Christ, even though they despised him. Even his own parents were afraid to support him. He spoke the truth and did not care that those in power had inflicted a further indignity upon him by kicking him out of the synagogue. When Christ appeared to him and told him who He was, he worshiped Him, almost certainly falling at His feet in gratitude.

This man will be in the kingdom of God because he believed in Christ. But there is more to say. It would be surprising if this man did *not* live the rest of his life faithfully serving the Lord. If so, we can only imagine what he will be like in the kingdom. What an example of the power and grace of God he will be for all eternity! A man who went from a poor despised beggar to a man of great honor and authority in the eternal kingdom of the Son of God. The Lord's words that the "works of God will be displayed in him" will seem like one of the greatest understatements of all time.

When the religious leaders put this man on trial, they called him a disciple of Jesus (John 9:28). They meant it as a slur. If he continued following Jesus, he would continue to experience difficulties because of his association with Him. He would continue to be a religious and social outcast. The One he was following would eventually be executed as an enemy of both Israel and Rome. No doubt he would be reminded that God had struck him with blindness because of sin and that being a disciple of Jesus was just further proof that he was outside the will of God. Many that met him would continue to believe, and point out, that he was a notorious sinner.

But what the religious leaders meant as a slur, he would take as a great compliment. He could be a disciple of the King of kings. When looked at in that light, there is no doubt this man would say he was glad for the thirty-five years he lived in physical blindness. He was glad for his poverty and the pity he experienced from those who saw him begging. He was glad for the accusations of his neighbors and even the religious leaders that he was a sinner who deserved what he had had to endure. In light of the eternal rewards he would enjoy as a disciple of Christ, his sufferings, which we consider unbearable, would seem light indeed.

The same is true for Elisabeth—and for any believer who faithfully endures hardships for the Lord. As they honor their Lord in the midst of their difficulties, they know not only that they will live with Him forever, but that He will also reward them beyond anything they can even imagine.

Let's see what the New Testament says about these rewards.

CHAPTER FOUR

A Communistic Eternity?

Many Christians mistakenly believe they will spend eternity in an environment surrounded by clouds, the way heaven is pictured in cartoons that depict believers with harps and wings. Yet the Bible tells us that believers will dwell forever on a new physical earth, not among the clouds in the heavens. In the last book of the Bible, the Apostle John describes the new earth on which God's people will dwell (Revelation 21:2). It is a tangible place with cities, streets, trees, and nations. The description even mentions a river (Revelation 22:1).

The idea that we will be floating around the clouds gives rise to another false view of eternity—the view that everyone will be equal in that future day. Even though this concept hasn't worked on earth, people believe God will usher in a perfect communistic utopia in which everyone is exactly the same in every way.

If we think of the kingdom in this way, the utopian view makes sense. It is hard to picture why there would be any differences among millions of people if all they do is sit around on pillowy clouds playing harps. The most we could possibly say is that perhaps some could play their harps better than others!

This false idea of heaven, where everyone will be equal, just seems fair to many people. Certainly, God's fairness demands such a kingdom, they think—only in that kind of environment could everybody be happy.

But knowing that the eternal kingdom does indeed involve life on a new earth—and not in the clouds—opens our minds to the possibility that there will be differences among the inhabitants of that earth. Could it be that it will be a kingdom in which there are jobs to do and that different people will have different responsibilities? Do we dare suppose that the Lord, who will be the King of everything, will give different levels of authority to different people so that they can fulfill those responsibilities?

Again, many would naturally reject such notions. But with a little reflection, they seem reasonable. The idea of floating on a cloud forever sounds extremely boring, like an old cartoon I once saw of a person sitting on a cloud with a harp, and the caption, "I wish I had brought a magazine." If somebody had that view of eternity, it would be understandable why they would not desire for it to come any time soon!

Fortunately, that is not what the Bible says eternity will be like. Certainly, the kingdom ruled by Christ will be a place of excitement and joy—a kingdom whose subjects are working, serving others, and experiencing new things as they perform what the Lord wants them to do. This description is far more accurate (and exciting!) than the notion of playing a musical instrument in a misty heavenly environment forever.

Reason also suggests that there will be differences among those who live on the new earth. We all agree that God is just and fair, and with a little reflection, we can see that it would be blatantly *unfair* if everyone was equal in Christ's kingdom in every respect.

R. E. Neighbour, a Southern Baptist preacher of the early twentieth century, told a story about another famous Baptist preacher of his time. I. M. Haldeman was the pastor of the First Baptist Church of New York City. One day he placed two empty chairs in front of the congregation. He said that one represented a believer who cared little for spiritual things and lived to fulfill his own desires. The other chair represented a mature believer who endured in faithfulness in serving the Lord to the end of his life. Haldeman asked the congregation if both these believers would receive the same rewards when they entered into the kingdom. Haldeman's answer was, "Not so long as there is a just God in heaven!"[1]

Both Neighbour and Haldeman believed in the eternal security of the Christian. A Christian can never lose the gift of eternal life. But they also believed that a Christian could live a life that displeased the Lord. Such a believer would enter into the kingdom of God but would suffer the loss of rewards in that kingdom. That believer would not be great in that future world. He would not hold a position of great authority.

We could imagine, for example, that a martyr for the Christian faith will receive some kind of reward from the Lord when he enters into His kingdom. That outcome would be considered very reasonable and fair. Nobody would begrudge the martyr of whatever honor the Lord bestowed upon him. Even in this life, we recognize that those who are heroes should receive honors that the rest of us do not. Soldiers who die in battle for their country are even rewarded for their sacrifices in various ways. Their families, for example, are given special financial compensations. A Medal of Honor recipient should have privileges and rewards that the rest of us do not enjoy. And they do.

The same notion, in many different ways, exists in the fallen world in which we live. In principle, at least, those who work hard and obtain certain benefits and privileges are seen as having earned such things. A person who works long hours to establish a business should enjoy the financial benefits of such work. A lazy person, who only lives for his own pleasure, does not experience such blessings—nor should he.

Of course, in the final analysis, it does not matter what we think is right or just. What do the Scriptures say about this subject? Will the Lord promote those who have faithfully served Him when He comes and establishes His kingdom? Will those who faithfully endure suffering for Him experience any kind of reward for doing so?

---

[1] R. E. Neighbour, *If They Shall Fall Away* (Miami Springs, FL: Conley and Schoettle, 1984), n.p.

Elisabeth with her entire family when she is five years old. We were living in Hawaii on an army installation.

Angels Teach Us the Answer Is Yes

Perhaps the holy angels are an example of what the kingdom will be like for believers in this regard. The Bible tells us that there is an innumerable number of these beings (Revelation 5:11), but it also tells us they have different roles and degrees of authority. Before he fell into sin, Satan, or Lucifer, was an especially powerful angel, evidently part of a higher order of angels called the cherubim (Ezekiel 28:14).

Other cherubim among the ranks of the angels are described in detail in Isaiah 1:5-11. They appear to have a role that requires them to be near the Lord. In the book of Revelation, John sees four living creatures performing such a function. These are probably cherubim (Revelation 4:6-8).

Isaiah the prophet describes another type of angel, the seraphim, who have the privilege of being particularly close to the throne of God (Isaiah 6:2-3). Their name might suggest that they are responsible for proclaiming the holiness of God.

One particular angel is unique in the Bible. Michael is the only angel called an "archangel" (Jude 1:9). The word means "a ruling angel." Perhaps he took over that role when Satan fell into sin. He is also said to have the special privilege of serving as the protector of God's chosen people in the Old Testament, Israel (Daniel 10:13-21). This passage also speaks of other angels who are "princes." Some of these angels appear to have responsibilities in the affairs of the nations on earth.

Throughout the New Testament we find that certain angels are given different roles. Gabriel has the honor of announcing the birth of John the Baptist to his father and the birth of Jesus to Mary. He seems to be a special messenger for the Lord. Some are what can be called guardian angels in some sense (Matthew 18:10). At least a few angels were given the high honor of ministering to the Lord after He fasted for forty days (Mark 1:13). Angels are said to minister to human believers in some way (Hebrews 1:14). In the book of Revelation, angels are given different jobs in the last days.

We are not told why Michael is a ruling angel and others are not, or why Gabriel is chosen as a special envoy for God. How did certain angels obtain the high positions of cherubim and seraphim when the majority did not? Why do some have the title of "prince" but others do not? Even though we do not have the answers to such questions, it is clear that there are different levels of authority among these unfallen creatures.

In the coming kingdom of God, believers will at least in some ways be like the angels (Mark 12:25). Like them, we will no longer sin, so we will not feel jealous if others have a higher position of honor in the kingdom. The rest of the angels certainly do not resent the archangel Michael or the special messenger Gabriel because they are not given these positions themselves. At the very least the angels teach us that God would not be unjust to put into place, in His kingdom, positions where believers will differ from one another in the roles and honor they will have in eternity.

Different Rewards

The New Testament teaches us that in God's kingdom He will give crowns to some believers, but not all. Surely these crowns represent some kind of authority or privilege in the kingdom of the Lord. Martyrs for the faith will receive a special crown (Revelation 2:10), as will leaders in the church who faithfully perform their duties (1 Peter 5:4). Clearly not all believers will be martyrs. Not all believers serve in leadership positions in the local church.

Paul says we should live our lives as believers in such a way to receive a crown that not all will receive (1 Corinthians 9:24-25). Believers who long to see the Lord, and live their lives in a way that reflects that desire, will also receive a special crown (2 Timothy 4:8).

In addition to these special distinguishing crowns, Jesus said that some in that day will be richer than others in certain ways. He commanded His disciples to lay up for themselves treasures for that day (Matthew 6:20). Believers can actually do things that invest in eternity. Even the smallest good deed, such as giving a glass of water in service to others, will warrant a reward from the Lord (Matthew 10:42).

Many think that working for rewards, or even desiring them, is selfish. But Jesus *commanded* His followers to do so. He *wants* to reward His children. He wants them to have positions of honor in His kingdom. It will honor the King to reward His servants in this way. Whatever the Lord commands cannot be selfish. In a similar way, even in this world, parents enjoy giving rewards to their children when they do well.

It is not sinful to desire rewards in Christ's kingdom. In fact, the author of Hebrews tells us it is sinful *not* to desire to be rewarded by the King. He says that if we want to please Him we must believe that He will reward those who diligently seek the things that please God (Hebrews 11:6).

No wonder, then, that one of the last things Jesus said to His followers in the Scriptures is that He will reward them for their good works. He promised that He will come soon, and when He does, He will pay them for the good they have done. Specifically, He said that when He comes, He will bring His rewards for His people with Him (Revelation 22:12). He will not forget the works they have done for Him.

The bottom line in all of this is that some will be greater in the kingdom of God than others. The twelve disciples, who spent more time with the Lord in His earthly ministry than anybody else and heard Him teach daily, clearly understood this principle. One day, they were arguing among themselves about which of them would be the greatest. It is interesting that Jesus did not rebuke them for that kind of thinking. In fact, He confirmed that some will be greater than others. He did rebuke them, however, for trying to obtain this greatness in the wrong way (Mark 10:35-44).

In many of His parables, the Savior taught the same truth. When He comes and reigns, some of His servants will rule over ten cities, while others will rule over five, and still others will not be given this kind of authority at all (Luke 19:12-27).

We know that when He returns, Jesus Christ will rule over everything. He will be the eternal King over a kingdom that will never end. It is not surprising, then, that the degree to which His children were faithful and obedient to Him will determine to what degree they will have the privilege of ruling with Him. This life is preparing believers for the role they will assume for all eternity. As one of my favorite Bible teachers once said, "This life is training time for reigning time."

Being great in the kingdom of God is all about being like Christ. The more a believer is like Him in this life, the more he will be rewarded in that day. This changes the whole idea about rewards. The believer who wants to be great in the kingdom is desiring to be more like His King and Savior. It is the Father's will that we become more like His Son. The believer who is greatly rewarded is one who lived his life in such a way that the world saw Christ in him. Such a life honors the Lord. In His grace, He has determined that a life that brings honor and glory to Him will result in great reward.

How great a prospect is that? What greater goal could a believer have than to become more like the One who loved him and died in order to give him eternal life as a free gift by faith alone? What purpose in this life could be greater than hearing Him say, "Well done, good and faithful servant!" (Matthew 25:23). We cannot fully grasp the joy such a believer will have on that day as the Lord glorifies Himself by making believers like that great in His kingdom.

But how are such lofty goals realized? How can we, as believers, become more like the only perfect Man who ever lived? Every Christian who is honest with himself recognizes how far short he falls of this goal. One thing is for sure: we cannot bring about that change in our own power. It will take a miracle.

The Lord has made a way for that miracle to take place: by giving the believer the Holy Spirit at the moment of faith in Jesus for eternal life. God's Spirit must accomplish the work of transforming us into the image of Christ.

There is another truth here, though, and it is a truth that is harder to accept. If we want to be like Christ, we must walk like He did. He experienced great difficulties in His life. About seven centuries before Christ was born, an Old Testament prophet said that He would be a "man of sorrows," and One who would be "acquainted with grief" (Isaiah 53:3). Certainly, when we read about His life in the pages of the New Testament, we see that these prophecies were fulfilled. Nobody suffered like He suffered.

On more than one occasion, the Lord told His disciples that if they wanted to be like Him, they too would have to endure great difficulties. Nobody wants to experience such things, but the exciting thing about them is that *God uses them to make us more like His Son* (Matthew 10:24; Mark 8:34-38; Luke 6:40; John 15:20; 2 Corinthians 4:8-17). If we want to be more like Christ, we will go through hardships. How comforting to know that when we do, we are, in a small way, walking in His footsteps. If we allow Him, the Spirit of God will use these things to make us more like Him.

But we must be honest with ourselves. Only a masochist would welcome even a small portion of the difficulties Christ experienced. How could we hope to endure such things? No doubt, it is through the supernatural power of the Spirit of God who dwells within us. We cannot do it on our own. Just as we were saved from hell because of the grace of God, when we believed in Jesus for that gift (Ephesians 2:8-9), we need His grace to endure the hardships that are necessary to become more like Christ.

Elisabeth modeled that for me. In His grace, God used the hardships she endured to make her more like Christ.

Elisabeth, on the Christmas when she was 15.

CHAPTER FIVE

His Grace Is Sufficient

Most people who study the New Testament consider the Apostle Paul a hero. He endured a great deal of suffering as the result of his work for the Lord, and his ability to do so seems almost superhuman. In fact, it was.

Travel in the first century was a difficult and dangerous endeavor. Yet, this man traveled around the Mediterranean world by foot and sea for years, planting churches wherever he went. The message he proclaimed was promoting a religion that was not legal in some of the places he went, and he was confronted by people who opposed his work at every stop. His own people considered him a traitor and an apostate from the religion of his fathers.

After being involved in this kind of life for around ten years, he was compelled to defend himself to a church he had planted years before. Even in this church, there were people who strongly opposed him. In response, Paul wrote them a letter describing the hardships he experienced as a servant of the Lord.

The list of these things is long and impressive. During those ten years he had received thirty-nine lashes from Jewish religious authorities on five different occasions. I picture him with a broken and bleeding back, the way movies I've seen depict slaves in the Unites States who were beaten with lashes.

But that was not all he went through. Three times, he had been beaten by rods. While traveling on the Mediterranean, he was shipwrecked three times, an event that often resulted in death. On one of those occasions, he spent a night and day in the water, the whole time not knowing if he would be rescued. On his very first missionary journey, the locals stoned him and left him for dead. He had been imprisoned on more than one occasion.

In all of his travels he faced danger from robbers and from his many enemies, among both the Jews and Gentiles. He spent many nights hungry, thirsty, and exposed to the elements, stating that he was often in danger of death. At the beginning of his ministry, the Jews in a particular city convinced the local king to try to put Paul to death, and the apostle had to be let down the city wall in a basket and flee for his life (Acts 14:19-20; 2 Corinthians 11:24-33).

When I read such a list, it is hard to comprehend. I don't know how he did it. When he wrote this letter to the church in the city of Corinth, he was not a young man. He was probably nearing the age of sixty, and by first-century standards would have been considered elderly. How was he able to continue to endure such things? Why didn't he retire from his work and go back to his hometown, being content with his contribution to the Christian church? I think most Christians have the same reaction I do when I consider this man's life. Just one of the beatings he went through would have convinced me to find another way, a more comfortable way, to serve the Lord.

We know that Paul was a tentmaker by trade. I am fairly confident that just one experience of receiving thirty-nine lashes would have compelled me to take up that honorable line of work full time. I would have worked extra hours as a tentmaker and financially supported somebody else, somebody younger than myself, to do the missionary work I had left behind!

While I stand back and can only admire from afar what Paul went through, I find I can more easily relate to what he says to the church at Corinth next. He talks about another difficulty he faced, one that he was dealing with as he wrote the letter to them. He refers to it as a "thorn in the flesh" (2 Corinthians 12:7).

We do not know what this thorn was, but most people who study Paul's life agree that it was some kind of physical ailment. There are indications that he was not a healthy man (Galatians 4:15). The beatings he took during his Christian ministry would have amplified any physical problems he may have had, and these things may have made his travels even more difficult. One could think of severe arthritis, for example. Others have suggested that Paul was dealing with the lingering effects of malaria, which was common around the Mediterranean Sea.

A very popular opinion is that the thorn in Paul's flesh was vision loss. Older people may automatically think he had cataracts. Perhaps his difficult travel conditions, which resulted in a poor diet, had contributed to the progression of the disease.

This condition would be hard for anybody, but for someone in Paul's line of work, in the first century, it would have made ministry especially difficult. Simply for the sake of argument, let's assume this is the illness that confronted him.

I can relate to the way he first responded to this difficulty. I try to imagine being in his shoes, after suffering all he did for the work of the Lord, and now having to deal with the prospect of going blind. Surely, I would think, God would want to heal me of this ailment so that I could continue planting churches in the Roman world and be more effective in doing so. A blind, or nearly blind, missionary would be severely hampered in that work. Besides, Paul was in the process of writing many of the books that would make up the New Testament. That work would be much easier if Paul could see!

That appears to be what Paul thought as well. He did not ask the Lord to take away his imprisonments, his nights spent in hunger, or even his beatings. But he explains how he did ask the Lord to remove this thorn in the flesh. In fact, he asked Him to do it on three different occasions (2 Corinthians 12:8). That is exactly what I would have done!

Paul had witnessed many healings in his time of service to the Lord. In fact, he himself had healed many sick people of their diseases and had even raised a dead man to life (Acts 19:11-12; 20:7-12). He knew God could heal him of this "thorn." My guess is that he expected that He would do so.

I can also imagine his initial disappointment when God told Paul that the thorn in the flesh would remain. However, whatever he felt, God did not leave him in despair over his condition. His difficulties would not prevent him from doing what God wanted him to do. This was true whether it concerned writing letters or traveling around the Roman world to plant churches. As the Lord put it to His servant Paul, *"My grace is sufficient for you, for My strength is made perfect in weakness"* (2 Corinthians 12:9).

It was not the answer Paul wanted. But it was one that he embraced. Paul was a man who proclaimed the grace of God—a grace that had the power to give eternal life to everybody who believed in the Son that the Father had sent for that gift. It was a power that raised His Son from the dead and would do the same for every believer. It was a power that would soon bring in an eternal kingdom of God.

What God was saying to Paul was clear: Paul was a messenger of this grace and power. What greater way to proclaim that message than to live it out? In his physical weakness, whatever that thorn may have been, God would give him the strength to do great things for Him. It would be clear that Paul was not doing these things in his own power. All those who saw him and heard him preach would see a man who was supernaturally empowered. God's grace was more than sufficient for the tasks that faced Paul. Paul would become a walking billboard for that power and grace. God would take a weak Paul, do great things, and thus magnify His strength. The prefect way to do that was through a Paul who had to rely on that strength.

No wonder, then, Paul responded the way he did to the answer he received from God in regards to his thorn in the flesh. Since Paul's greatest desire was to glorify God, what better way to do that than to let God's strength be magnified in his weakness? As a result, Paul said he would brag about his weaknesses. Whatever his physical problems were, he would be proud of them!

The reason he could feel that way is because those problems allowed him to experience the power of Christ resting upon him. Because of that power, it was only when he was weak that Paul was truly strong (2 Corinthians 12:9). Paul would live by the power of the risen Son who dwelled within him.

Talk about a hard lesson! Paul is saying that the power of God is most clearly seen in a human vessel that is going through difficulties. In such a person, others can see what that power can do. We can look back at the life of Paul and see what God did with such a weak vessel. How great was his powerful Savior!

That was certainly the case with Jesus Himself. One could not be in a more physically weak condition than He was on the cross. He had been brutally beaten with a lash. He wore a crown of thorns. His friends had abandoned Him. He had been betrayed by one of those closest to Him. He had been unjustly condemned by His own nation, as well as the Romans. Naked, He was nailed to a piece of wood. He experienced the cruelest of deaths.

But what power was displayed in all that weakness! In His shameful death, the Son of God took away the sins of the world. His death ensured that every believer in Him would receive eternal life, a life that could never be lost. In His death, He conquered death itself, the greatest of all enemies. Such power and grace could only be seen through the hardships Jesus endured, through His weakness.

Paul was able to comprehend that God's power is most visible when it works with what is weak. God accomplishes great things in weakness.

But that was Paul. We have a tendency to think somebody like him was on a different spiritual level than the rest of us. Is it even possible that God could do the same with people like me and the believing readers of this book? Could others going through hard times become pulpits from which the grace and power of God are loudly proclaimed?

Surely, the answer is yes. Paul would never say that what he experienced was only available for special people like him.

Many believers can testify to times in their lives when they were able to show others the grace and power of God sustaining them in times of difficulties. For a moment of time, my wife and I were a part of that group of believers. I ask that you indulge me as I speak of what happened.

It Is Not Just for Paul

When Amy and Elisabeth were born, we were told there was a good chance that they would not survive. The first seventy-two hours were critical. If they lived through the first three days, their chances of living improved considerably. Pam and I focused on that seventy-two-hour timeline, a short-term goal that we so desperately wanted to reach. Our prayers were focused on that goal. We didn't really think about what long-term health problems the twins might have as a result of their prematurity.

The girls, of course, were in the pediatric ICU. There were certain hours we could visit, and each visit was an ordeal. We had to go through rigorous hand washing and wear protective clothing. We weren't allowed to hold either girl, but we could touch them and talk to them. They had tubes and different monitors attached to various parts of their bodies. A nurse was assigned to each baby and was always standing next to their beds to take care of any need and to answer any questions we had.

The girls were tiny. Amy would eventually drop to about one and a half pounds, and Elisabeth two pounds and four ounces.

As the second day of their lives was nearing its end, we were encouraged that we were going to reach the goal we were praying for. The last opportunity to visit them was at 11 p.m. Pam had delivered the girls by C-section, so she was still in the hospital. After visiting the girls, we went up to Pam's room and fell asleep.

About two hours later, around 1 a.m., the door to Pam's room opened and the light of the hallway streamed through. The light, along with the voice of the girls' doctor, woke us up. She told us we needed to come down and see Amy. In my half-asleep and confused state, I explained to her that we had just done that, at the regular scheduled visit time. I was assuming she thought we had forgotten the hours of visitation and missed an opportunity.

As I was assuring her that everything was OK, she cut me off. She said, "Mr. Yates, Amy has suffered a massive brain hemorrhage. I don't think she is going to survive the night. You and Mrs. Yates need to come say goodbye to her."

It is strange how I reacted to her words as though they did not register. I think Pam reacted the same way. I guess I simply thought the doctor was mistaken. Maybe, due to my young age, I couldn't conceive of something like that happening. More importantly, I had *just* seen Amy, and she was fine, all things considered. Almost to placate the doctor, we got up and started toward the ICU. Pam was still sore from the C-section, and we had to take the elevator. I don't remember anything being said on that ride. I am sure I was thinking that once we got there, this whole mess would be straightened out. Maybe I thought the doctor had confused Amy with another baby.

From the cleaning station, we couldn't see the girls. But after scrubbing our hands and putting on the proper clothes, Pam and I were led to Amy's little ICU bed. Whatever denials were running through my head from the moment the doctor had opened the door of the room upstairs quickly evaporated as we were confronted with reality. Some of the tubes had been removed from Amy's body. There was blood all over the white sheet she was lying on. Most noticeable of all was her color. Her skin had turned what appeared to be black. I suppose it was a very dark blue.

The nurse was standing by, and I first asked her about the color. She said that because of the brain hemorrhage, Amy's blood was not able to carry oxygen throughout her body. I didn't understand how that worked, but simply accepted it.

I then asked her about the blood. She said that in order to release some of the pressure on Amy's brain, they had to do a spinal tap. That caused the blood to spill onto the sheets of her ICU bed.

I didn't understand the mechanics of that either. But I did understand one thing: the doctor was right. Amy was not going to make that third day. She would die that night. In fact, I was not sure she hadn't already died. She was black and was not moving, except for any movements the machines attached to her were causing.

It was also clear to Pam and me that we were there to say our final goodbye to our daughter. The ever-present nurse left us alone to be with Amy by ourselves. There were other nurses in the room, as well as a few doctors. We were aware of their presence, but also aware that they were not there to provide any medical help for Amy. It was past time for that. There was nothing they could do for her. They stood at a distance and respectfully gave us time alone.

I know we were a pitiful sight. What human could see what we were going through and not ache for us? Prior to the birth of the twins, I had never even been in an ICU before. Certainly, I had never seen what I was seeing with my eyes.

Any parent will understand how Pam and I responded. We were standing at the side of a bed that held what we thought was the dead body of our daughter. We cried out to God to save her. We were crying. We realized that we were completely powerless. There was nothing we could do. There was nothing anybody in that room could do for us, even though they had years of medical training. The abundance of modern medical equipment surrounding us couldn't help us in our grief either.

As I stood at that bedside, I related for the first time to Paul's sufferings. Paul described his weakness as he dealt with his blindness. His ministry often led him to fear for his life. Every parent knows that what I am saying is true. I was hurting more than Paul was in this particular situation. I would gladly have become blind if Amy would live. I would gladly have traded my life for hers if I only had had the power to do so. But I didn't. At that moment, I understood exactly what Paul went through when he asked God to take away his thorn in the flesh. I understood how weak he felt.

I don't know how long Pam and I prayed and cried together there in the ICU. But I remember very clearly what happened. In the midst of this crushing pain, a change took place. As I recall, it occurred at the same time for both Pam and me. Our praying and weeping turned into singing. Neither of us are musically inclined, but we started singing to Amy all the old hymns we knew that spoke of God's love and how Christ had conquered death. We calmly told her that God loved her and that we did too. We told her that even though we were going to miss her, we were happy for her because she was going to the One who loved her more than we did. We went from crying out to God not to take her, to telling her it was OK to go.

My grandfather, who had been a believer, had died a few years earlier, and we told her to say hello to him. We told her we couldn't wait to see her in the kingdom of God, and how different she would look on that day! There would not be any machines or bloody sheets when we met again.

It may sound strange, but we went from profound sadness to rejoicing. We certainly weren't masochists, but we realized the same truth Paul did: God's grace was sufficient for us, even in this situation. We were in the presence of death, but Christ had defeated even this enemy. Such was the power of God. In our weakest moment, the weakest moment any parent could possibly face, that power could carry us.

Paul in his weakness said that in those moments the power of Christ dwells in us (2 Corinthians 12:9). Is it too much to say that what happened in that ICU was an example of such power? Pam and I believe we will live forever because we have believed in Jesus for eternal life. If we die physically, Christ will raise our dead bodies from the grave. That is power! Never in our lives had we ever preached that message more clearly than in the ICU during those early morning hours. The doctors and nurses who saw and heard us saw that we had placed our hope in the One who would raise Amy. He was with us. Because of Him, the horror that was before us was not the final chapter. His power was magnified in our weakness, and that power allowed us to respond as we did.

We stayed with Amy that morning, not knowing what was going to happen. Would somebody come and tell us that she was officially dead? Would they ask us if we wanted to remove the rest of the wires and tubes? In any event, that is not what happened. Instead, slowly, Amy's color returned. She would make it to the third day. We were told that her brain had suffered damage, but they didn't know the extent of it.

That was hard news to accept. But we, like Paul, had learned a valuable lesson: God's grace and the power of Christ are more than sufficient for whatever circumstances we find ourselves in.

I wish I could tell the reader that I always remembered that lesson. I wish I could say that whenever I faced difficulties after that day I always relied on God's grace and power to sustain me and direct my perspective. Unfortunately, if I said such things, that would be a lie.

But there was somebody there with us in the ICU who lived out these truths in a much better way than I did. Elisabeth was in the bed next to Amy when all of this occurred. Of course, she was not able to understand what happened to her twin sister at the time. But she would later hear the story. She took the lessons Pam and I got a glimpse of to heart. She learned them in spades. Since weakness would characterize every part of her entire life, she had the opportunity to rely on the grace and power of God in remarkable ways. She had the same experience as Paul. I, and many others, had the privilege of seeing the power of Christ dwelling in and transforming her. To see such things was to witness a miracle.

CHAPTER SIX

Seeing a Miracle Take Place

Many of us have tried to envision ourselves in the New Testament stories of Jesus' miracles. We can only imagine how we would have reacted to seeing Him walk on the Sea of Galilee, turn water into wine, or give sight to the blind.

The reaction of people who saw Him do such things varied. Some were amazed. Some gave thanks to God. Some believed in Him as the Christ. When He cast two thousand demons into a large herd of pigs, the whole region became gripped with a "great fear" (Luke 7:37). On the other hand, the religious leaders were jealous and accused Him of being possessed by an evil power that allowed Him to do such things.

But I am confident that one reaction was universal, even among His enemies. I can almost see it in my mind. The display of His power certainly left mouths opened, agape in amazement. In the history of the world, people had never seen a man do what He did.

The greatest display of power in Christ's ministry was His power to raise the dead. Once, the Lord stopped a funeral procession on the way to the cemetery, and a large crowd saw Him tell the dead man to arise from the coffin. It is easy to imagine all the open mouths in the crowd when the dead man sat up and spoke. Luke tells us that fear gripped all of them, they glorified God, and they spread the news about what they had seen to all the cities around them (Luke 7:11-17).

On another day, the Lord raised a little twelve-year-old girl from the dead, and her parents saw her get up and walk. In one of the greatest understatements of all time, we are told they were "greatly astonished" at the power they witnessed and what it had done for them (Mark 5:42).

When Jesus raised His friend Lazarus after he had been dead for four days, reactions varied. Many believed in Him as the Christ, seeing such a clear display of the power of God. Some, even though recognizing that power, out of jealousy planned to kill both Him and Lazarus (John 11:45-51).

It is left to our imagination what it must have looked like when the Lord raised Himself from the dead and walked out of the tomb. We are told that just the glory of the angel, His messenger at the tomb, caused a group of soldiers there to faint from fear (Matthew 28:4)—surely His own glory was even greater than that. Later, His post-resurrection appearances to the disciples evoked fear, amazement, and worship.

None of us have ever seen with our own eyes the power that could cause a body to rise from the dead—we can only see it through the words of the Scriptures—but we can assume we would have responded similarly. And the New Testament tells us that the same power that raised Lazarus, the little girl, the man in the coffin, and the Lord Himself, is ours as well. It is the miracle of resurrection power.

The Scriptures make it clear that the Holy Spirit was the source of that power. When the Lord began His ministry, the Spirit came upon Him at His baptism (Mark 1:10). In His first sermon, He proclaimed that the Spirit was upon Him and His ministry would be characterized by miracles done in that power (Luke 4:18).

Believers today often do not realize it, but that same Spirit dwells within them. On the night Jesus was arrested, He told His disciples that He would send the Spirit to them after He died. The Spirit would dwell in them permanently. The doctrine of the Trinity tells us that God is One, but He exists in three Persons—the Father, the Son, and the Spirit. Jesus and the Spirit are one. When Jesus tells the disciples that He will send His Spirit to them, He tells them that He Himself will be with them (John 14:16-18).

On the Day of Pentecost, this promise of the Lord was fulfilled. The Spirit fell upon the disciples in the upper room they were in (Acts 2:1-4). Paul would later write that all who believe in Jesus for eternal life have the Spirit as well (1 Corinthians 12:13). Every believer can proclaim that the Spirit, and thus Christ, dwells within them (Romans 8:9-10).

It is not an exaggeration to say that this means that the power that can give life to the dead lives within the believer. Paul specifically states this: "If the Spirit of Him who raised Jesus from the dead dwells in you, He who raised Christ from the dead will also give life to your mortal bodies through His Spirit who dwells in you" (Romans 8:11).

What is Paul saying? The believer in Christ has the same power that raised Christ from the dead. It is the same power Christ used to raise others from the dead. But none of us have raised a body from the dead. We have never even seen it done with our own eyes. Can we actually believe that such power lives in us?

To understand what Paul is saying, we must look at the dead body he says can be raised. It is *our* mortal bodies. We live in bodies that are dead (Romans 7:24). Clearly, Paul is not saying we live in physically dead bodies. What he means is that our physical bodies are not able to do anything that pleases God. Paul says it like this: "In me, that is, in my flesh, nothing good dwells" (Romans 7:18). The physical bodies of believers cannot produce spiritual life and peace by themselves. In very simple terms, we would say that our mortal bodies are unable to produce the fruit of the Spirit. In that sense, they are dead.

But the Spirit of God, who dwells in the believer, can produce this life in our "dead" bodies. We can experience this kind of resurrection from the dead.

This sounds so philosophical and hard to understand—perhaps because what he is saying is hard to believe. In straightforward terms, Romans 8:11 clearly states that believers can experience a kind of resurrection miracle.

Many Christians read such statements and think such wonderful things are not for "average" believers like us. But the teaching of Paul is clear: Christ, through His Spirit, lives within the one who has believed in Him for eternal life. The resurrected Christ can now live through each believer and demonstrate His power in the works the Spirit performs in our dead bodies.

Another way of putting it is that as believers walk by the Spirit, the Spirit makes them more like Christ. How incredible is this promise! In our dead bodies, the risen Lord can work and be seen at work in us. The world can see the resurrected Christ in us as He makes us more like Him.

When we read the Word of God, we see the Lord and His glory in its pages. We learn what He desires of us and, in His example, what He wants us to be. Our dead mortal bodies could never attain that, but the Spirit of God can. In 2 Corinthians 3:18, Paul puts it this way: "But we all, with unveiled face, beholding as in a mirror the glory of the Lord, are being transformed into the same image from glory to glory just as by the Spirit of the Lord."

When I see the image of the glorious Lord in the New Testament, I realize how far I fall short. How could any of us hope to be transformed into His image and become more like Him? It almost defies belief. Paul says it would take the power that raised Christ from the dead to accomplish a work like that in the life of His children.

Just like every believer, I can accept by faith that such resurrection power exists, even though I did not see Jesus' resurrection miracles with my own eyes. But I have an advantage in this area that many other believers don't have. Even though I have never seen a physically dead body rise from the grave, I have seen that resurrection power at work in another kind of dead body. In fact, I got to see it for more than thirty years.

Like all of us, Elisabeth lived in a spiritually dead body. It was incapable of producing fruit pleasing to God. From a human perspective, this inability was even more graphic in Elisabeth's case. Physically, her body was weak and incapable of even doing what the world would consider beneficial. In many ways, she was unable to do common, non-miraculous things. But what a miracle the Lord accomplished in her. In *that* body, I saw the resurrection power of the resurrected Lord at work as He made her more like Him.

In a very real way, her physical limitations caused that power to shine forth in an even more glorious way as we saw what her King did in her. The weaker the vessel, the more clearly the power of the risen Lord is seen. As Paul told us, strength is perfected in weakness.

CHAPTER SEVEN

How Did He Do It?

How does the power of the Lord through His Spirit make a believer like Elisabeth more like Christ? By leading that believer in paths like those in which He walked. A believer is somebody who has believed in Jesus for eternal life. But not all believers are disciples. A disciple is a believer who desires to be more like Christ. Inherent in the word "disciple" is the idea of following the Lord. It means to be a student. A disciple is one who learns things from the Lord. As the disciple walks in the footsteps of Christ, He teaches him the things he needs to know. He uses those experiences to make the disciple more like Him.

A person does not have to be a Bible scholar to understand that Christ walked a difficult path, just as the Old Testament prophets said He would. His whole life was filled with hardship, eventually culminating in His execution. From a human perspective, the difficulties Christ went through allowed Him to learn to trust in His Father during those times. They taught Him, experientially, the physical cost of obeying His Father in those situations (Philippians 2:8; Hebrews 5:8). He learned patience and endurance through physical pain, which taught Him to look beyond the difficulties to the world to come (Hebrews 12:2). His suffering also enabled Him to understand what His followers would go through when they themselves went through hard times.

It should not surprise us, then, that when we see a believer who is like Christ, we will find that he or she has been through difficulties. The Spirit used these experiences to cause this transformation.

But what kind of difficulties are we talking about? What kind of hardships can the Spirit of God use to make a believer more like Christ?

It's Not Just Persecution

Sometimes, when we think of the Christian life, we tend to focus on only one kind of difficulty, which is persecution. We admire believers in foreign countries who are imprisoned or even executed because of their faith. It is easy to see that such believers, who are faithful in those circumstances, are walking in the very footsteps of Christ. After all, Jesus was persecuted for what He preached, and none of us would argue that a believer who experiences such suffering and rejection for doing the same will be rewarded for doing so when Christ comes.

We all have heard about people like that. The Bible itself is full of such examples. We admire people like Stephen in Acts 7, who was stoned to death because of His faithfulness in teaching the truth about the Lord in the midst of such strong opposition. Paul suffered as a missionary for preaching about Jesus, and also paid for it with his life. The New Testament is full of references to Christians punished by governmental authorities for simply practicing the Christian faith.

Believers through the ages have suffered and continue to suffer for the same reasons. They have been imprisoned, tortured, separated from their families, and even killed, especially in countries with authoritarian or communist leaders. For example, Watchman Nee, a Christian leader in China, died in prison after twenty years of captivity. Many who served with him experienced the same fate. One can read about his life and see how he learned patience and endurance during the things he went through. It was not difficult to see Christ at work in him as he trusted Christ through his sufferings.

But is it only these kinds of difficulties that the Spirit can use in our lives? Many Christians, especially in the West, will never be subject to such things. What about the hardships the "average" believer goes through, such as the loss of financial security or health, the loss of a family member, or even the struggle against sinful desires? Can the Spirit use these to teach us to rely on the strength of the Lord and to become more like Him? Can we faithfully endure such things, giving thanks to the Lord for teaching us what we need to know, and being grateful that the Spirit is making us more like our Savior in the process? What about the hardships Elisabeth endured? She was never imprisoned or tortured for her faith, but she went through many other kinds of difficulties.

With just a little reflection, the answer to these questions is obvious. Hardships, difficulties, trials, and sufferings can come in many different forms—and however they come, they provide an opportunity for the child of God to learn to trust in Christ. They provide a chance to focus upon the world to come as we realize the temporary nature of our sufferings. They give us an opportunity to show the world our dependence on Christ, just as He depended upon His Father.

Fortunately, this is not just an opinion. The Bible tells us that afflictions used by the Spirit of God in the life of believers can come in various stripes. In Romans 8:16-17, Paul talks about suffering for Christ. Later, he gives a list of things that can cause suffering: tribulation; distress; persecution; famine; nakedness; peril; and sword (Romans 8:35).

It seems certain that the words "persecution" and "sword" point to sufferings that faithful Christians experience in certain situations because of their faith, like Watchman Nee did in China and Stephen and Paul did in the New Testament. The "sword" is a picture of the power of governments to inflict such punishment (see Acts 12:2 and Hebrews 11:37). This sword has been used to kill faithful believers, and is still used that way today.

But the other words Paul uses to describe sufferings are broader. The word "tribulation" is like that. In Acts 7:11, it describes what people go through when they don't have enough to eat. In 1 Corinthians 7:28, married believers are said to experience tribulation as they cope with supporting their families. Leaders in the church go through tribulation when there are disagreements in the church (2 Corinthians 2:4). Believers going through financial scarcity do as well (2 Corinthians 8:12). James says that the lives of widows and orphans experience "tribulation" because of their social and economic circumstances (James 1:27). Many women will heartily agree when the New Testament says that when a woman gives birth she goes through "tribulation" (John 16:21).

While persecution and tribulation both cause suffering, there is a difference between them. The Lord Himself distinguished between a believer who is persecuted and one who experiences tribulation (Matthew 13:21). Paul is saying both can be used to make the believer more like Christ.

The word "distress" in Romans 8:35 also describes many things that can cause suffering in the life of the disciple—any stressful situation in a person's life. The Old Testament used it to describe the feeling of facing danger (Isaiah 30:6). In literature written around the time of Christ, it was used to describe a tough financial situation or mistreatment by one's family. It is easy to see how a person going through a serious illness or relational difficulty, such as a woman abandoned by her husband, would experience "distress."

A person can live in a country that experiences a "famine" without going through persecution because of his Christian faith. The word itself, however, has the more basic meaning of being hungry, like the prodigal son, who had wasted his money and could not buy food but was willing to eat the food put out for the pigs he was caring for (Luke 15:17). Jacob and his family had to move to Egypt because of "famine," as there was much more food in Egypt than in their home country (Acts 7:11).

The words for "nakedness" and "peril" can describe a number of different things as well. A poor person in the Bible could be said to experience nakedness because he did not have enough financial resources to properly clothe himself. An individual could be said to be in peril because he found himself in a dangerous situation, the way we might feel today if we got lost in an unfamiliar city and wandered down a dark alley. Paul used it to describe how he had to be careful when he traveled because there was always a danger from robbers. Anybody who succumbs to a serious illness would find himself in peril as well. Once again, a person does not have to be persecuted by political authorities to face trouble.

In an earlier chapter, we saw how Paul described his sufferings for Christ when he experienced a thorn in the flesh. Such sufferings allowed him to enjoy the power of God at work in him. In 2 Corinthians 12:10, he lists many different kinds of sufferings. A few of them are the same words used in Romans 8:35, but he adds some new ones: "infirmities;" "reproaches;" and "needs."

One with infirmity is going through a period of being weak, often because of illness. Paul's close friend Timothy experienced this because of a certain kind of stomach sickness (1 Timothy 5:23). In an interesting use of the word, Paul says that he first came to the church at Corinth with feelings of such inadequacy that he felt weak with infirmity (1 Corinthians 2:3). This probably refers to some kind of physical difficulty.

A "reproach" occurs when a person goes through any kind of hardship. In Acts 27, it is used to relate what happened when a ship wrecked on an island and lost all of its cargo. The damage that rain can inflict on property is also said to bring a reproach on the property owner. In modern terms, we could say that a Christian business owner who experiences a severe financial loss fits this description.

A believer can have "needs" in a number of different situations: the need for good health; relief from distress; or even the need for patience to endure difficulties. In 2 Corinthians 6:4, Paul uses the word to describe his need for patience in dealing with certain Christians in Corinth who were opposing his ministry. Here is an example of suffering with Christ that involved how other Christians treated Paul, not how the unbelieving world persecuted him! It was as if he was saying to Christ, "Lord, help me to serve Your people. I 'need' patience to do so." Perhaps some readers of this book have experienced these things when dealing with other believers in their church.

Another New Testament book also teaches us that sufferings can come in many different forms. James speaks of the trials Christians can go through as "various." The important thing to remember, according to James, is that the Lord can use such things to teach us what He desires for us, and those who allow the Lord to teach them in these circumstances will receive a crown from the Lord (James 1:2-12). What James is saying is that Christ can use these various hardships to bring about the kind of life He will reward.

At this point, it only needs to be said that in James 1:3, James says Christians should look upon the many different trials in their lives as sources of joy. Like Paul in Romans 8 and 2 Corinthians 12, these hardships can have a positive influence on the life of a believer. Paul agrees with James when he says that believers can give thanks to God for their difficulties because God can use them to produce the kind of character He approves of (Romans 5:3-4).

Because we live in a fallen world, difficulties are all around us. When we face them, we have two options: rely on the power of God or become bitter. When we rely on the grace of God, the Spirit can work in us during these times of weakness and make us more like the Lord.

Isn't that exciting?

Many Christians, however, especially those who live in countries like the United States, might read about suffering with Christ and conclude they do not have the opportunity to do so. In Mark 8:34-38, Jesus told the disciples that He was going to take up a cross and go to His death. He then told them to do the same. He was literally telling them to walk in the same footsteps that He was going to walk. They were to follow Him to Jerusalem, where He would meet that fate. If they followed Him, they would have to deal with the same people who killed Him.

But how many of us will ever come close to experiencing something like that? Few of us will ever experience persecution from the government or be tortured for their faith.

What About Elisabeth?

Elisabeth often felt that her physical limitations made her especially immune to such dangers and limited how she could serve the Lord. How could she boldly and publicly follow Christ in discipleship, when she couldn't even take a physical step on her own? She would never be able to literally walk in her King's path of suffering or learn the lessons of walking on that path. She would never even have the opportunity to show her willingness to suffer persecution for Him. She certainly couldn't pick up a literal cross and follow Him to Jerusalem.

But Paul and James make it clear that any believer can suffer with Christ. The Spirit of the Lord who dwells in every Christian can use many things to teach a disciple to trust in Him, to learn patience and endurance, to long for the world to come, and be transformed into the likeness of the Man of Sorrows. One of the greatest privileges I have experienced was seeing Him do that in the life of Elisabeth.

CHAPTER EIGHT

The Fruit of the Spirit

The fruit of the Spirit describes what the power of the Spirit of God can bring about in the life of the believer: love; joy; peace; endurance during suffering (longsuffering); kindness; goodness; faithfulness; gentleness; and self-control (Galatians 5:22-23). Parents who have sent their children to vacation Bible school or a Christian children's program like AWANA will probably recognize these words from a popular song the kids learned to sing.

This list shows we cannot produce these things in our own power. We cannot make ourselves people who are characterized by love and joy, kindness or gentleness. It can only take place as Christ transforms us by *His* supernatural power. When we look at Him in the pages of the New Testament, we see the perfect embodiment of all this fruit.

When we talk about Christ making us like Him, it is accurate to say that He produces in us the fruit of His Spirit. They are the same thing. To be like Christ is to display the work of His Spirit in us. Others can actually see it. Since it is the resurrected Lord Himself who is doing it, others can see the power of His resurrection in us.

This transformation can only happen as we walk on the paths He walked. He walks with us, but these paths involve difficulties, which are necessary to produce the fruit of Christ's Spirit in our lives. We see in His Word what He requires of us, and we rely on Him to make us what He wants us to be—more like Him. As we see Him in the Scriptures—His character and conduct—we are to ask the Spirit to produce that character and conduct in our lives. That should be our constant prayer.

Nobody enjoys going through any kind of difficulty. But it is only when the believer understands what Christ can do through them that we can see them in the right perspective. We can have joy as we go through them, as James says, because our Lord is using them to make us more like Him.

But there is another reason these difficulties can be a source of joy. In the world to come, Jesus is going to rule over everything. He will be the King of kings. He will have all authority. And as discussed earlier, there will be differences in His kingdom—some will have greater authority than others. Logic tells us that those who share authority with the King will be those who were most like Him. The New Testament teaches us this as well. Those who will be great in the kingdom are those who are like the One who is the greatest of all.

That means when a believer goes through difficulties and asks the Lord to use such things to make him more like Him, *that believer is asking to be great in His kingdom*. All believers will be *in* the kingdom of God; none will be excluded. Eternal life cannot be lost. But the Lord desires that His children be *great* in that kingdom. He wants every child of God to become more like Him.

Have you seen Christians who were gentle and kind? Have you seen believers who loved other Christians and patiently endured trials, relying upon the Lord to accomplish His will in them? If so, you were seeing the resurrection power of the Lord at work in them. Those difficulties played a great role in making them like that. Believers who live like that will be great in Christ's kingdom. No wonder James says we should consider it joy when we go through difficulties!

One of the most famous sermons the Lord preached is known as the Sermon on the Mount. It is the first of the Lord's sermons recorded in the book of Matthew, and He gave it to His disciples. At the very beginning of the sermon, the Lord told them how they could be great in His kingdom: by having certain characteristics, those that reflect His own character. But such characteristics can only be attained through hardships. Greatness in the Lord's kingdom will be given to those who were made like Him through their trials. Knowing this is the key to understanding the message of the Sermon on the Mount.

It begins in Matthew 5:3-12.

Elisabeth and Amy getting ready for their prom. They were 20 years old.

CHAPTER NINE

Those Who Are Blessed

We often hear Christians use the word "blessed." In the Bible, it has the basic meaning of being happy. People who are described as being happy are people who are being shown favor by God. The world, and unfortunately many Christians, think God's favor is marked by such things as health, career success, a great marriage, and a nice house. We can almost hear somebody say, "I got a new job today. I sure am blessed!"

The prevalence of this attitude was evident in the account of the man born blind. He had none of these kinds of things, so his community, and even the disciples, concluded God was not pleased with him. He or his parents must have sinned. Most would say he was certainly not blessed.

As we might expect, Jesus did not agree with that assessment. In the Sermon on the Mount, Jesus listed nine things that show that God's favor is on a person—known as the Beatitudes—and He repeatedly said that those who exhibit these nine things are blessed (Matthew 5:3-12). Clearly, those Jesus called happy are not those that the world considers happy.

In Galatians, we saw that the Spirit produces things like peace, gentleness, kindness, and goodness (Galatians 5:22-23)—strikingly similar to the traits Jesus named in this famous sermon. We could say that the fruit of the Spirit and the Beatitudes are basically describing the same thing.

In the sermon, the Lord declared that the meek, the merciful, and the poor in spirit are blessed—similar to the fruit of being gentle and kind. It is easy to see how a kind and gentle disciple of the Lord would be one who is meek and merciful to others.

According to Jesus, those who are blessed are acquainted with suffering. It is not the person with a great job or a big house that are called happy, but those who "mourn" and are "persecuted" for their faith.

These two words (mourn and persecuted) imply that difficulties are needed to produce godly character in the life of a believer. In the Sermon on the Mount, Jesus was speaking to the original disciples, who would indeed experience persecution for their faith—in fact, most of them would eventually be put to death by the ruling authorities. Such persecution would lead to much mourning in their lives.

Once again, we see a connection here with the fruit of the Spirit: one who mourns finds himself in a situation where the Spirit can produce longsuffering. But, as we have seen, Christians go through other kinds of difficulties that lead them to mourn and to develop the character described in the sermon.

Elisabeth is a case in point. And such believers are just as "blessed" as the original disciples.

A believer who "hungers and thirsts for righteousness," or has the "pure heart" Jesus spoke of in His sermon, can be said to demonstrate the fruit of the Spirit called goodness. Perhaps the easiest seen connection between the fruit of the Spirit and the Beatitudes is the fruit of peace. The Lord says that the favor of God rests upon the "peacemaker."

Even a quick reading of the Beatitudes shows us that someone who has such traits is like Christ Himself. It is not surprising that we find such similarities with the fruit of the Spirit, for only His own Spirit can produce these qualities in the life of a believer. We would certainly say that a person who is like Christ is a happy person upon whom we see God's favor.

Being like Christ is enough reason to be called blessed. Jesus was the perfect fulfillment of all the Beatitudes. Nobody was poorer in spirit than the One who humbled Himself and rode a donkey into Jerusalem to offer Himself as their eternal King. He was certainly pure in heart, gentle, meek, merciful, and righteous. He knew what it was like to mourn and to experience persecution from those with political and religious power. He was, as Isaiah the prophet predicted centuries before His death, "a Man of sorrow and acquainted with grief" (Isaiah 53:3). Nobody was as meek as the One who left His throne in heaven and became a man in order to die upon a cross. In fact, Jesus used this very word to describe Himself when He said, "I am meek and lowly of heart" (Matthew 11:29).

Nobody had a hunger and thirst for a righteous kingdom to come like He did (Hebrews 12:2). Nobody was as merciful as He was, shedding His blood so that we could have the forgiveness of sins. Nobody was as pure of heart as He, since He was the sinless Son of God. Nobody was a peacemaker like He was, offering eternal peace with God to all who believe in Him (Romans 5:1).

But people with these characteristics are not only blessed because they are like their Savior. The Lord says that they are blessed because they will be great in His kingdom. As we have already seen, this is what we would expect. Those who are like the King will be rewarded in His kingdom. In the Beatitudes, the Lord says that such people will not only be *in* His Kingdom—they will *own* it (Matthew 5:3). They will not only be *citizens in* that kingdom—they will actually *inherit* it (Matthew 5:5). A person who gains an inheritance in something actually becomes an owner of what he inherits. Lest we miss Jesus' point, He makes it clear at the end of the Beatitudes. We should note that He said that those who are like Him will receive a great reward in the kingdom of heaven (Matthew 5:12). Those who exhibit the characteristics described in the Beatitudes, those who show the fruit of the Spirit, will be rewarded.

The word for "reward" is important here. It refers to something a person receives for work that is done. Specifically, it describes the wages a worker is paid when he works. Think of it as a paycheck an employee receives at the end of the month. The Lord says that the believer who is faithful to Him will be paid for the work he does for Him, like a worker is paid for a job well done.

This is a major theme in the Sermon on the Mount. Jesus, the greatest teacher who ever lived, was telling His disciples in perhaps His most famous sermon who will be great in His kingdom. Specifically, He told them about being wealthy in that day. In the very next chapter, the Lord told the disciples:

> "Do not lay up for yourselves treasures on earth, where moth and rust destroy and where thieves break in and steal; but lay up for yourselves treasures in heaven, where neither moth nor rust destroys and where thieves do not break in and steal" (Matthew 6:19-20).

If we remember that Jesus was speaking to the disciples, who already had eternal life, we see that He was telling those who already believed in Him that they could be rich when He returns to rule. Some will be richer than others. Some will be greater and have more authority. Believers have the opportunity to lay up treasures, to invest, in the coming kingdom by how they live their lives. Certainly, those with much treasure in that kingdom will be those who were like the King. They did what He told them to do, and the character of the King was produced in them. How appropriate to call them blessed!

It is not surprising that Jesus' last message to His followers involved the same message He gave in the first sermon in Matthew. The theme of being rich is found in both places. In Revelation 22:12, the Lord tells the church that He is coming soon. When He comes, He will pay them for the work they have done:

> "Behold, I am coming quickly, and My reward *is* with Me, to give to every one according to his work."

It must be kept in mind that our eternal salvation is not the result of our works. Our eternal salvation is a gift that has nothing to do with our works. Paul says that in Ephesians 2:8-9:

> For by grace you have been saved through faith, and that not of yourselves; *it is* the gift of God, not of works, lest anyone should boast (emphasis added).

When we believe in Jesus for eternal life, we receive it as a gift. It is given by grace. What Jesus said to the woman at the well bears this out. He tells her that eternal life is the gift of God and that He can give it to her. He also tells her once she has it, she can never thirst for it again. It can never be lost. He compares believing in Him for that gift to taking a drink of water:

> "...but whoever drinks of the water that I shall *give* him will never thirst. But the water that I shall *give* him will become in him a fountain of water springing up into everlasting life" (John 4:10, 13-14).

What Jesus offers this woman is the very definition of grace!

But this is not what the Lord is describing in the Beatitudes in the Sermon on the Mount. It is extremely difficult to be kind to others, to be patient, to be a peacemaker, to live righteously, and to suffer through difficulties. That involves a *lot* of work. But when we are honest with ourselves, we realize none of us can do these things in our own power. Nobody can look at the Beatitudes and not realize we need God's help if we hope to be described in those terms. It would take supernatural power. Christ must produce these traits in those believers who seek to be like Him, and those blessed people display the character of Jesus in their lives.

Have you ever seen the Lord do that in someone? I have seen such a person with my own eyes. And just as the Lord taught us, the difficulties in her life played a large role in what I saw.

CHAPTER TEN

Blessed Are the Poor in Spirit

(Matthew 5:3, 5)

As the Lord taught us, two of the characteristics that make a believer blessed are that he is "poor in spirit" and "meek." It appears that these two are related. Maybe being poor in spirit focuses on the attitude one has toward God, while being meek focuses on the attitude one has toward others.

The idea of being poor in spirit sounds strange to modern ears. What did the Lord mean? Most commentaries agree that it describes somebody who is humble, who doesn't think too highly of himself or consider himself better than others. To be poor in spirit is the opposite of arrogance.

It is easy to see how the Lord could use a life full of difficulties to produce this kind of attitude in a believer. Trials show how fragile and temporary life is. Difficulties can give us empathy toward others who experience hardships. A Christian who goes through such things can come to the point where he understands he must rely on the power of God and not on his own strength. That is exactly what Paul learned when he experienced his thorn in the flesh.

It is interesting that on another occasion the Lord gives a similar sermon and He makes the point that difficulties can go a long way in helping a disciple become poor in spirit. In Luke 6, He simply says that the *poor* disciple is blessed (Luke 6:20). While it is true that a believer can become poor in spirit without going through financial difficulties, it is more likely that one who is financially poor will become so. In those hard times, the Lord can teach him to rely on Him and not on his own resources.

This is what James means when he says that it is often the poor believer who is *rich* in faith (James 2:5). The poor believer has the privilege of seeing how Christ sustains him during his times of need. This, in turn, can make him poor in spirit. Certainly, he is humble when he considers his relationship with God.

In some versions of the Bible, the word "meek" is translated "gentle." The connection between being poor in spirit and being meek is obvious. Perhaps we could see the difference in that being poor in spirit leads to being gentle. A meek, humble person is considerate and gentle with others, especially those in need—because he realizes his own need to rely on God. He naturally understands when others are in need of help as well. People like this do not see themselves as too important to be kind to others. The meek person is one who finds it easy to think of others in need and serve them.

I don't think it is an accident that Jesus mentions that those who "mourn" are blessed as well (Matthew 5:4), and that He puts this Beatitude between those who are poor in spirit and meek. To mourn involves feeling sadness over some situation or life's circumstances. Believers who mourn over these difficulties can understand the difficulties others pass through and can, as a result, be meek or gentle with them. This is especially the case when we remember that the Spirit is teaching and transforming the child of God to have such empathy.

A Biblical Portrait

The connection between mourning over difficulties and being poor in spirit can be clearly seen in another Biblical account. Two Gospels tell the story of a woman who had been hemorrhaging blood for twelve years (Mark 5:25-34; Luke 8:43-48) and had endured tremendous hardship as a result. In that society, her condition made her religiously unclean and she was viewed as a sinner. Anyone she touched would also be unclean and would have to undergo a ceremonial bath. Her social ostracism was evident every day as her neighbors would steer clear of her and warn her not to touch them. Like the parents of the man born blind, many would have considered her as one being punished for some sin. She too was a religious outcast.

But her troubles included other realities. We are told that she had experienced financial ruin because she had spent any money she had on doctors, none of whom could help her. Although the Bible does not say it, we can confidently assume she was alone. If she had been married, her husband would almost certainly have left her. In that culture it was easy to put a wife away, and her husband would have had many good reasons for doing so in the eyes of the Law: to continue living with her would have resulted in financial and social ruin and would have also hindered the practice of his religion. He would have been in a constant state of uncleanness if he remained with her.

On top of all that, the loss of blood would have had a terrible effect on her health, eventually leading to her death. In the ancient world, this woman found herself in dire straits. In fact, she had no hope and would have had resigned herself to that fact. She was a picture of one who had every reason to mourn.

But her fortunes would take a miraculous turn. She heard about Jesus of Nazareth. From the accounts, we can conclude that she believed He was the Christ. The Old Testament, her Bible, had said that when the Christ came, He would be able to heal the sick. She had heard about how He had cured countless others of their illnesses. She would go to Him.

When we read her story, it becomes clear that her hardships, her reasons for mourning, had turned her into one who was poor in spirit. She knew Jesus could heal her, but she also knew that she was not worthy to be in His presence. In her mind, He would certainly not have the time, nor the desire, to deal with her on a one-on-one basis. Like her neighbors, this One sent from an infinitely holy God would definitely not want to touch her.

But in her despair, and with no other option, *she would touch Him*. She did not even consider that He would lay His hands on her to take away her illness. That would make Him religiously unclean, and the possibility that He would do that for her did not even enter her mind. She wouldn't even ask.

She had heard His touch could heal and that is the way He had healed many others. But she was different. She saw herself as completely unworthy of such contact with anybody, especially the Christ. Instead, she would try to touch the very edge of his clothes. She would do it in a way that He wouldn't even know she was there.

This thinking was not only the product of her inability to have human contact. It probably also reflected a common superstition in the first century that a mighty faith healer's ability to heal was transferred to his clothes. She understood the greatness of Christ and saw His clothes as magical. She believed that the power of Christ was such that even His robe would be able to do what all the doctors she had seen were not able to do. Her belief in magical clothes was misplaced, but she certainly understood and believed in the power of Christ.

Her humility is evident throughout the story. If the large crowd surrounding Jesus had known her condition, they would have yelled at her to leave. How dare she even think she was worthy to be there as a functioning member of society? After twelve years, she had become accustomed to this way of thinking and agreed with it. She must approach Him in secret. As she made her way through the crowd, she went up *behind* the Lord. She did not want Him to know she was there because she saw herself as unclean. In secrecy, she reached out her hand and touched the hem of His robe. We can only imagine the adrenaline that was racing through her body as she did so.

The Gospel writers tell us that she immediately knew she had been healed. The natural response of such a miraculous deliverance would have been a shout of joy and a desire to share the good news with those around her. But even here, her poorness of spirit is seen. Luke tells us she simply wanted to escape without notice (Luke 8:47). She only wanted to slink away, unnoticed in the crowd that surrounded the Lord. The Christ had made her well, and in her mind that was more grace than she could ever have expected. It was certainly more than a person poor in spirit expected.

But she would receive even more from the One who is *full* of grace.

Jesus knew somebody had been healed by touching Him. He wanted to know who it was and asked that the person identify himself or herself. We are told that the woman came in fear before Him, no doubt expecting Him to rebuke her. What would He say when He realized that such an unclean person as herself had dared to touch such a godly and important Person? In her fear, she thought perhaps He would even "undo" the healing. He had the power to curse her with some other malady. As a person poor in spirit, she probably expected that is what she deserved, especially after touching Him.

Instead, Jesus wanted to know who touched Him because He wanted to *talk to her*. He wanted to teach her. He wanted to let her know that it was not her superstitious belief in magical clothes that had cured her. Her faith in Him as the Christ would have resulted in eternal life for her. Her faith in His power to heal her—not the fabric of His clothes—was the source of her deliverance from her sickness.

He did not rebuke her. In fact, He called her "daughter," clearly a term of endearment. How surprising that must have been to the ears of this woman! For years she had been rejected by her neighbors, religious leaders, and probably her husband. But the Christ wanted to help her understand and disciple her. The King of kings cared about somebody as undeserving as her.

After this encounter with the Lord, this woman disappears from the pages of the New Testament. But in at least some regards we can be fairly certain what happened to her. I feel confident that she remained poor in spirit, and I imagine that when Jesus continued teaching in Galilee, she would have often been in the crowds listening to His words.

A Modern Portrait

In some ways, this woman's life paralleled Elisabeth's. Elisabeth had reason to mourn over her circumstances. Her physical limitations meant she would not be able to do what most people can do and resulted in great discomfort and pain. But it was truly a miracle to see how through these things she too became someone who was poor in spirit and meek.

The clearest example of this in my memory occurred when she was around fifteen years old. In the morning, Elisabeth, Amy and I would wait for the school bus, and when it arrived, I would strap Elisabeth and her wheelchair in the back. Amy would sit on the seat across from her. There was a girl, a few years younger than Elisabeth, who rode in the back with her. This girl got on a stop or two before Elisabeth and Amy did. She used a special chair because her cerebral palsy was extremely severe. She was blind and could not communicate. It was also obvious to me that she was unaware of her surroundings. She was very small for her age due to the severity of her cerebral palsy. Her body was basically straight and completely rigid. My guess is that she could not bend any of her joints.

One morning as Elisabeth, Amy and I got on the bus, this girl was screaming in what might be described as a cross between a yell of pain and fear. It seemed she had no idea what was going on. Maybe something was hurting her. It was impossible to tell. This screaming went on the whole time I was loading Elisabeth into the bus and strapping her in. We were right next to the girl and I felt very uncomfortable.

I am ashamed to admit that I was irritated at what was happening. I resented the fact that my daughters had to sit next to this girl and hear her scream on the way to school. I wondered why the parents of that girl had not kept her home that day, or why they even sent her to school at all. She obviously could not understand anything they would teach her. I was pretty sure that at school they would have just put her in a corner somewhere, hoping she would simply be quiet.

I also remember being eager to get off the bus so at least I wouldn't have to hear the wailing of that girl. I certainly had more important things to do.

After securing Elisabeth's chair, I turned to exit the front of the bus. As I was walking down the aisle, I heard the voice of Elisabeth. She said, "Don't worry. I will be your friend." I looked back and saw her stretch out her arm, with much difficulty, and touch the other girl's hand. The girl stopped screaming and was calm.

My daughter and I had completely different attitudes on the bus that morning. Our actions reflected those attitudes. How clear was it which one of us demonstrated the character of the One who preached the Sermon on the Mount?

Blessed are those who mourn. The Spirit of God can use such things to make them poor in spirit. These are those who are humble before God. The Spirit can use such things to make them meek, those who are gentle with others. The King is looking for believers like that. They are the ones who will be great in His kingdom. And they should be, because they are like the King. In fact, you could say He was there on the bus.

CHAPTER ELEVEN

Blessed Are Those Who Hunger after Righteousness

(Matthew 5:6, 8)

The Lord also says in the Sermon on the Mount that those who hunger after righteousness and those who are pure in heart will be great in His kingdom. Just as there was a connection between those who are poor in spirit and those who are meek, it seems there is a connection here as well. Being righteous and being pure seem to be related. Perhaps we could say both imply loving what is good.

The Lord probably gives us a hint at what it means to be pure in heart. Later, in the Sermon, He says, "Where your treasure is, there will your heart be also" (Matthew 6:21). The pure in heart is one who looks for the coming kingdom of God. His heart, or affections, are not in this present world.

The pure heart is not contaminated by the things of this world. It does not live by this world's standards. In this world, those who are successful are valued and envied, not those who mourn. Humility and gentleness are not hot commodities.

Those who hunger after righteousness are those who want to be more like Christ, who was perfectly righteous. To hunger after righteousness would include longing to see His kingdom, where sin will be no more and righteousness will reign (2 Peter 3:13).

Those who hunger for righteousness and those who are pure in heart are looking for a new world. Just as mourning can lead to humility and gentleness, so mourning can lead to these qualities as well. In this new world that is coming, where righteousness dwells, the things that cause mourning will be things of the past.

But the Lord says more than this about these two characteristics. Those who hunger after righteousness "will be filled" (Matthew 5:6). Here is a wonderful promise. Those who want to be more like Christ will become more like Him in this life. The Spirit will make that believer more like Him, but only through the power of the resurrected Lord.

The same thing is true for the pure in heart. Jesus states that such a believer will "see God." While all believers will be in the kingdom, those who are pure in heart and look forward to that coming kingdom will "see" God at work in their lives. Once again, they will see the power of the resurrected Lord changing them. They will see it in their own lives and others can "see" it in them as well. As a result, the pure in heart will find that their minds become more and more uncontaminated by the standards of this world.

It is no wonder that mourning in this world can be used by the Spirit of God to bring about these miracles. A believer going through difficulties often finds it easier to live for, and long for, the world to come.

I mentioned earlier how Elisabeth often spoke about her longing for the Lord to come back. She looked for His kingdom. Paul said there will be a special crown given to those who look forward to that day. It would have been easy for somebody with Elisabeth's disabilities and struggles to become angry with God. But such struggles can also have the opposite effect. The Spirit of God can use them to produce gratitude for the Lord's promise that such afflictions are temporary since they only belong to this fallen world, which is passing away. Jesus promised that He will bring a righteous kingdom, and when He comes such afflictions will be no more. The pure in heart are looking for that day.

Elisabeth had this attitude. A little while after becoming a believer, when she was around ten, she was going to the store with her mom. As they were driving, Elisabeth out of the blue said, "Mom, I am going to miss you." Pam found that to be a strange statement. After all, Elisabeth couldn't go anywhere without our help. So, Pam asked her, "Libby, where are you going?"

Even at that young age she showed that the Spirit of God was working in her. She said (and this is almost a direct quote), "Mom, my body is not like yours and Dad's. I am not going to live as long as you all will. But that is OK. I look forward to the day when I see the Lord and He gives me a new body. I just wanted to let you know that even though I am excited about it, and am looking forward to that day, I will miss you."

Through the years, Elisabeth would express this same sentiment. Occasionally, she would bring up the topic in our conversations. She would ask what the Bible says about the resurrection or what I thought it would be like in some particular detail. Her response was invariable, even in her teenage years.

To understand how she reacted, you have to know a characteristic of cerebral palsy. When a person with cerebral palsy gets startled or excited, they cannot control their movements. It is like their body jerks. If one of us was feeding Elisabeth and somebody suddenly came up behind us, Elisabeth would have a startle reflex and her whole body would jump. Many plates of food were lost in this way.

When Elisabeth would hear a verse about the promises of the Lord's coming kingdom and what it would mean for her, or when I would tell her what the Bible says it will be like, she would respond that way. She would hear about the coming righteous kingdom in which things like cerebral palsy would no longer exist. In her excitement, her whole body would jerk and become stiff. The best way to describe it is that she would practically jump in her wheelchair. Her head would go back and she would let out a squeal. And she would say, "Dad, I just can't wait!"

After her funeral, Elisabeth's aunt told us about her last conversation with Elisabeth. It was during Thanksgiving and the two of them were just talking about life in general. In typical Elisabeth fashion, she spoke to her aunt about what she was thinking. She told her that she was really looking forward to "going home" and seeing the Lord.

My guess is that most readers of this book are like I am. While I know that Jesus is indeed coming back, I don't have that level of excitement about it. The topic of the coming righteous King and His righteous kingdom is not in the forefront of my thinking on a constant basis.

How many ten-year-olds do we know who live with that kind of thinking? How many teenagers long for the things of this world to pass away and to be replaced by a new world? How about even a woman in her twenties? It literally takes a miracle to produce such longing in the heart of a believer. I think that is why we see it so rarely. But the Spirit can use something like cerebral palsy to affect such a miracle.

I had never had the privilege of living with somebody like that until Elisabeth came along. When I think of those conversations with her, I cannot help but think of the Lord's words: "Blessed are the pure in heart and those who hunger and thirst for righteousness!"

CHAPTER TWELVE

Blessed Are the Merciful Peacemakers

(Matthew 5:7, 9)

When the Lord described believers who are blessed because they will be great in the kingdom of God, He spoke of two other characteristics they must have. One is that they must be merciful. The other is that they must be peacemakers.

Those who are merciful will receive mercy (Matthew 5:7). All believers will stand before the Judgment Seat of Christ. Everyone at this judgment will be a believer who is already in the kingdom. This is not a judgment, then, to see if a person "goes to heaven." Instead, as we have seen throughout the Sermon on the Mount, it will determine rewards in Christ's kingdom. The Lord will look at each believer's works to determine what rewards he will receive, and how great he will be in Christ's rule.

Which one of us on that day would like to receive mercy? When we look at our lives, every one of us realizes we have fallen short in so many areas. If our desire is to be like Christ, we all recognize the impossibility of attaining that goal. We will all want Jesus to treat us mercifully if we want to gain His approval when we stand before Him.

If we hope to be great in His kingdom, we will certainly need that mercy!

I heard a true story of a man who received a speeding ticket. Because of how fast he was going, he was facing a steep fine. In hopes of reducing that fine, he decided to appear before a judge. The judge had a lot of experience with people coming before him to get out of paying their fines. Usually, they came forward to argue why their tickets were unjust, insisting the officer had made a mistake when he gave them a ticket.

As this man appeared before the judge, the judge thought that was what would happen. He asked the man, "Did you come here for justice?" The man said, "No, I came here for mercy." The man recognized that he was guilty. He did not want to receive what he deserved. He hoped for leniency.

When we stand before the Lord at His Judgment Seat and He looks at our lives, how can we obtain mercy? The Lord tells us. If we have been merciful towards others, He will be merciful to us. In other words, how we have judged others will determine how He will judge us. Jesus will specifically state this later in the Sermon on the Mount: "For with what judgment you judge, you will be judged" (Matthew 7:2).

We rightfully understand that being merciful means that when others wrong us and ask us for forgiveness, we give it to them. Part of being merciful is the recognition that we all sin. A merciful person does not hold others to a standard that he himself does not keep.

But being merciful involves more than forgiving others who wrong us. It involves an attitude that does not think of oneself as better than others. An unmerciful person does not give mercy, in part, because he thinks he is better than others. He does not forgive because he thinks the other person does not deserve his forgiveness. At the most basic level, an unmerciful believer sees the person needing forgiveness as beneath him. Unfortunately, Christians can be, and often are, unmerciful.

The Lord gave a parable illustrating the kind of attitude we must have if we are to be merciful. In Luke 18:9-14, He described how two men went to the temple in Jerusalem to pray. One bragged in his prayer about how much better he was than the other man. He listed in his prayer all of his good and religious deeds. The man did not see his own need for God's mercy or the need to extend mercy to others. Jesus Himself summarized this man's attitude by saying that this unmerciful man looked upon the other man with contempt (verse 9).

The attitude of the other man was the polar opposite. In his prayer, he did not see himself as even being worthy to pray. He definitely did not see himself as better than the other man, who was looking upon him with contempt. How beautiful is his simple prayer: "God, be merciful to me!" This is a clear picture of a merciful man.

In the little book of James in the New Testament, James also talks about those who will receive mercy from the Lord at the Judgment Seat of Christ. James says mercy will be given to those who have shown mercy to others (James 2:13). But James also concentrates on the attitude of the merciful person. Such a person does not think of himself as better than others. He has concern for the poor and the needy (James 1:27). In light of the hardships that the poor experienced in the world in which James lived, we could say that the merciful person is one who helps others who are going through afflictions.

James also says that the merciful person does not treat the rich man who comes into the church better than he does a poor man (James 2:2-3). It is human nature to treat people who can benefit us in a better way than those who cannot. A merciful attitude does not produce such thoughts or actions.

One can easily see the connection here between a merciful person and one who is gentle or humble toward others. As with all the Beatitudes, difficulties can be used to form these qualities in the believer. These difficulties give us empathy and allow us to see our own need for God's mercy and extend it to those around us. As with all the Beatitudes, the Lord can use struggles in our lives to transform us into merciful people.

That was certainly the case with Elisabeth. You would not have to spend much time with her to come to the conclusion that she did not think of herself as better than others. She did not look on others with contempt. She did not desire to be around smart, important, or rich people more than people who were not. Like the day on the bus, in dealing with a girl that her father did not want to deal with, she could say, "I will be your friend."

The reader will probably not have any difficulty in accepting those statements at face value, based upon what I have written about Elisabeth. After all, it might appear easier to develop such an attitude when you are in a wheelchair and dependent upon others for all your needs. Such a life may very well keep a person from getting a big head.

But it will probably be much more difficult to believe what I am about to say about her merciful attitude towards others. No doubt, many will say that I am naïve, or even worse, lying. But here it goes. In thirty-five years, I *never* heard her speak ill of anybody.

I would challenge the reader to think about what Elisabeth's life was like. Think about the cruel things people may have said about her in public or in high school. Think about how others did not even notice her when they were around her. How they talked to her parents instead of her because they thought she could not talk. Think about how, as she got older, girls her age would make friends and make plans with others while excluding her. Think about the doctors who, at least on some occasions, did not help her pain when we took her to them for help. The list, of course, could go on and on.

Now, think about what miracle must have taken place for her not to hold a grudge against those who treated her in those ways. When I say that I never heard her hold others in contempt, even if they might have deserved it in her eyes, I mean that literally. Some may say those are just the words of a father speaking, and maybe they are right. But I have had many tell me the same thing about her. Maybe there were times when she was alone, in the secret recesses of her mind, when Elisabeth struck out at the mistreatment she received from others. If so, I can only imagine that she would later have asked God to be merciful to them—and, like the humble man in the temple that day, asked God to be merciful to her as well.

It is not that I am exaggerating or blind when it comes to Elisabeth's character. It is just hard for us to believe because we are not used to seeing miracles occur right in front of our eyes. We have never seen a resurrection after all, and that is what I saw. What I am saying is that the resurrected Lord transformed my daughter into the merciful person I am describing on these pages. His power brought it about.

What is a peacemaker?

Just as there is a connection between being "poor in spirit" and being "gentle," there is also a connection between being merciful and another of the Beatitudes—that of being a "peacemaker" (Matthew 5:9).

A peacemaker, of course, is somebody who desires peace. In the context of the Sermon on the Mount, this would refer to believers who need to be reconciled after some kind of disagreement. Harmony between them needs to be restored.

Just as James tells us what a merciful person is like, so he tells us what a peacemaker is like. It is not surprising that according to James, the peacemaker is one who is merciful. The one who makes peace is one who does not think too highly of himself. He does not have selfish ambition. He is gentle with others (James 3:16-18). When there is a lack of peace among Christians who are arguing with each other, it is almost always the result of each one thinking too highly of his position or himself. If reconciliation is to take place, a dose of mercy towards the other one is needed. The peacemaker is one who models gentleness and mercy in how he deals with others. Others can emulate this attitude.

The Lord says that peacemakers are blessed and will be called "sons of God" (Matthew 5:9). In the New Testament, there is a difference between being a "child" of God and being a "son" of God. There are different Greek words used to describe this distinction. In simple terms, a child is a baby, and a son is a child who has matured. We could say that a son is a child who has grown up and looks and acts like his father. It is like when we see a young man who reminds us of his father and we say, "You can tell that is Bob's son. He acts just like him!"

All believers are the children of God. Everybody who has believed in Jesus for eternal life has His life and will live with Him forever. But the merciful Christian peacemaker has grown up. He is a mature believer whose actions reflect those of his heavenly Father. He will be called the son of God. The Lord is gentle and merciful toward us, and when we treat others in that manner, people can say we are just like our heavenly Father. In very simple terms, when others see a believer like that, they say, "I see Christ in him."

If you find a merciful believer, you will find a peacemaker. It will not surprise the reader to learn that Elisabeth was a peacemaker. She spent her life among folks in the church. I must warn you, here comes another statement that will be hard to believe. In all the churches in which we were involved, and in the life of our family, I can never remember a time when Elisabeth instigated dissension. Her gentle and merciful spirit simply would not allow her to do so.

When I look at my own life, and the times when my selfish ambition led me to enter into various conflicts with other believers, I recognize that Elisabeth was different. The Spirit of God had produced in her a character that I often did not, and do not, possess. It is not overstating the case to say that I actually observed a miracle.

I am not saying this to appear falsely humble. It simply means that Elisabeth was an example for me. The risen Lord had made her like Him. I could look at her and say, "I really see Christ in her." Anyone could spend time with her and think: Blessed are the merciful peacemakers, for they shall be called the sons of God.

CHAPTER THIRTEEN

Love: The Missing Characteristic

If the Beatitudes describe a believer who becomes more like Christ, there is a glaring characteristic of the Lord that is missing at the beginning of the Sermon on the Mount when the Lord lists those characteristics. That characteristic is love. Jesus told His disciples that if they were to be like Him, they would have to love one another (John 13:34). Jesus was God in the flesh, and John tells us that God is love (1 John 4:10). A life transformed by the resurrected Lord living through him will be characterized by love.

As is well known, the Biblical word for love in these verses is not a feeling. When it says that Christ *loved* us, it means that He desired what was best for us. That is what it means to love somebody. When John 3:16 says that God loved the world, the same thing is true. He sent His Son so that all who believe in Him would have eternal life. This is the greatest example of desiring what is best for others.

Parents know exactly what this means. Even with our faults, we love our children. We want what we think is best for them. The way most parents treat their children is probably the clearest example of what the Bible means by *love*.

It is not surprising, then, that when Paul lists the fruit of the spirit, "love" leads the list (Galatians 5:22). If the Spirit of God is working in a believer, He will produce love in him. A Christian simply cannot be like Christ if he does not love others.

John tells us that loving others will play an important part at the Judgment Seat of Christ. We could say that when the Lord rewards His children for how they lived, whether they loved others or not will be the most important factor as to how much they will be rewarded on that day. John boldly says that if the believer does not love his fellow believers, he does not love God (1 John 4:20-21). If we have not loved God, how can we expect to be rewarded by Him on that day? If we have not loved Him, how can we expect to be great in His kingdom? The answer is straightforward. If we have not loved others, we won't be.

Once again, we must realize that this has nothing to do with whether we are in the kingdom or not. Only believers will be at this judgment. If a person is at the Judgment Seat of Christ, he is already in the kingdom! This judgment will deal with *greatness* in His kingdom.

Even so, who among us can think about that day and not look upon it with fear? What will the Lord say to me? How can I hope to gain His approval when He considers my life? As we saw previously, being merciful to others will play a big role. But John plainly says that love will as well.

John talks about the judgment that will determine our rewards. He points out just how important our love for others will be:

> Love has been perfected among us in this: that we may have boldness in the day of judgment; because as He is, so are we in this world (1 John 4:17).

What John is saying is that God demonstrated His love for us in giving us His Son. When we as believers love one another, that love is perfected. As many have pointed out, the word "perfect" in the Bible often means something has matured. When a believer loves his fellow believers, he has matured.

Why? Because when we love others, we have become like our Savior! If that is the case, we can look forward to the Judgment Seat of Christ, because we were like the Judge! No wonder the loving believer can have boldness on that day. The One judging him will see Himself in that believer. We can have boldness because even though we recognize our many faults, we followed His example of loving others.

And that is what the Beatitudes are all about—becoming like Him. But it is strange that love is not one of the Beatitudes. Wouldn't it make sense for the Lord to say, "Blessed are those who love, for they will be great in the kingdom"? Why didn't He?

Well, actually, the Lord did. Just a few verses after the Beatitudes, Jesus tells the disciples that they are to love others. In fact, He tells them they are to love not only one another, but even their enemies (Matthew 5:43-44). If they did, they would be like their heavenly Father, because that is how He loves. In doing so, they would be mature "sons" of God (Matthew 5:45). The world would see them acting like the One who has given them birth from above. We could say others would be able to say that they were like their heavenly Father. Not surprisingly, then, Jesus says if a disciple loves others, he will receive a reward (Matthew 5:46).

When we look at the Beatitudes, we see that love is at the root of all of them. Those who hunger after righteousness and have a pure heart demonstrate a love for God in desiring that His kingdom come. The coming of the kingdom in itself is a desire for what is best for this world. Those who are poor in spirit, meek, merciful, and peacemakers demonstrate that they are seeking the good of others. They love others.

If we are talking about who is going to be great in the kingdom, all of this makes sense. If Jesus is going to be the King of the coming kingdom of God, who can expect to be great in His kingdom? Wouldn't it be those who are like the King? Wouldn't it be those who demonstrate the characteristics of the King? If there is any quality that characterizes Christ above all others, it would be how He loved others.

But to develop any of these characteristics, including love for others, it would take a supernatural work of God. As we have seen, this is true for all the Beatitudes. The risen Lord Himself would have to produce such things in a believer—and the process involves mourning and passing through difficulties, just as the Sermon describes.

When we see these characteristics in another person, we are seeing a miracle. How easy would it be for somebody like Elisabeth not to feel love toward the Lord because of her plight? He had allowed her to suffer with cerebral palsy. How easy would it have been for her to wish ill upon others so that they might have a greater appreciation of her own trials? How easy would it have been for her to be jealous of what others were able to enjoy in this life when she could not? In other words, it would have been easy for her *not* to love God and others.

Such a course of action would have been choosing to live by the flesh. That is what our selfish desires would produce. And that would be understandable in light of her afflictions. It would be easy to be bitter toward God and what she saw as the good fortune of others.

But looking back at her life, that is not what I saw. Her afflictions produced something else. I saw a young woman who loved God for what He had done for her in Christ. She loved the fact that His kingdom was coming, understanding that He was going to make all things new.

But the same thing was true when it came to others. Her own troubles gave her the ability to be gentle and merciful toward others. In the numerous prayers I heard her pray, she always desired what was best for others. She asked for the eternal salvation of unbelievers she met. She sincerely rejoiced when others received good news. In other words, she loved them.

Such things, in the midst of such hardships, can only come about by the work of the Spirit of God in a life. To see them is to see a miracle, a miracle of transformation. It was a miracle of resurrection power.

One day, Elisabeth will stand before the Lord at His Judgment Seat to determine how great she will be in His kingdom. I can't remember if she ever told me if she had boldness, fear, or a mixture of both when she thought of that day. But there is one thing I do know. I sure wish the Lord would allow me to stand in her shoes on that day.

CHAPTER FOURTEEN

How Can I Serve Others?

When we look at the Beatitudes and the fruit of the Spirit, we understand that the Spirit of God desires to produce in us the character of Christ. That is true for every one of the Beatitudes. As we have also seen, a major part of that process involves the difficulties we go through.

But if a believer is to become more like Christ, it is not only His character that is important. We should also do the things that He did. Our actions should imitate His actions.

Of course, this makes sense. If the Spirit produces the character of Christ in a person, it is a certainty that those actions will follow. If a believer is humble and merciful, and desires what is best for others, certain actions will become evident in his life.

Many have commented that the Gospel of Mark describes the actions of the Lord. In vivid detail, it records what Jesus *did*. It does so more than any of the other three Gospels that tell of the earthly ministry of Christ.

In Mark, if we were to speak about what Jesus did, we would use the word "servant." In fact, many say that the book of Mark presents Jesus as the "Suffering Servant of God." Jesus came to serve others. That is what He did.

At one point in the Gospel of Mark, the disciples wonder who will be great in Christ's kingdom. They thought such positions would be obtained by stepping over people and fighting their way to the top at the expense of others. In one of the high marks of the book, the Lord corrects their thinking. Many think these are the central verses of the book, summarizing what Jesus taught His disciples:

> Yet it shall not be so among you; but whoever desires to become great among you shall be your servant. And whoever of you desires to be first shall be slave of all. For even the Son of Man did not come to be served, but to serve, and to give His life a ransom for many (Mark 10:43-45).

It could not be more straightforward. If you want to be great in His kingdom, you must serve others. Jesus was a servant. For you to be great in His kingdom, the Spirit must develop that quality in you. If that quality describes you, you will do what the Suffering Servant did. You will do the work of a servant.

How did Jesus serve others? He healed those with illnesses. He told them how to have eternal life. He taught people how to live a life that resulted in the blessings of God. He told them how to receive eternal rewards. He displayed infinite patience as He taught the disciples amidst their many failures. He loved them all. Amazingly, all this service to others took place while He was in the middle of terrible difficulties. The Lord knew while He was serving people that He was headed to the cross. In fact, He kept serving them even when He was betrayed and nailed to the tree. He kept serving them by teaching and encouraging them. All of these actions sprung from His love for them.

When believers go through hardships, they may feel that serving others is not a high priority, or even possible. If Paul's thorn in the flesh was the danger of going blind, it would be easy to see how he would question his ability to serve others if he couldn't see. What good would he be to the churches he wanted to serve if he was disabled like that? But an even more fundamental question could have arisen in Paul's mind: since he was going blind, shouldn't others be serving *him?* Maybe his time of thinking of, and serving others, was over.

When Elisabeth heard sermons about serving others, she always had these questions. How could she serve others when others had to meet all of her most basic needs? She felt that she was *being* served, and thus doing the very thing that Jesus said *not* to do.

The problem with this thinking is it reflects a defective view of service. We often think we can only serve in the church if we are teaching, or going on a mission trip, or cooking for others, or some other kind of physical activity. If only those things qualify as serving, somebody like Elisabeth was excluded from serving others.

But she came to realize that she could serve others in different ways. The Bible says that Christ has given every believer a spiritual gift with which to serve the body of Christ, the church (1 Corinthians 12:7). One of those gifts is the gift of faith (1 Corinthians 12:9). It was obvious to me that that was Elisabeth's gift. It is my hope that the reader of this book is able to see that was her gift as well, by the things I have written about her.

In the midst of her difficulties and pain, she had an unshakeable faith that God was good. She demonstrated to others what it meant to have faith in God in the midst of hard times. She became an encouragement for others. She used her gift by becoming an example for others, including her dad. That was how she served them.

Even though she never verbally expressed it, it is obvious that she looked for ways in which she could serve the people in her life. At a fairly young age, she figured out that she could do it in very specific way: she could pray for others. And did she ever pray. If you ever wondered how her memory was, all you had to do was listen to her pray. She prayed for people I had long forgotten about. Her prayers were *long* because she prayed for *everybody.*

She would pray at length when she was by herself. She did not know we realized it, but after we had put her to bed and closed the door, it was very common to hear her pray in her room. Often, late at night, when I would pass by her door, I could hear her speaking. I would stop and hear her talking to the Lord about others.

She would also pray for certain things for herself. One of her most common requests was that the Lord would make her more like Him. As already discussed above, I had the privilege of seeing those prayers answered in many clear ways.

There was a final way Elisabeth served others. After she turned eighteen, she began to receive a disability check from the Social Security Administration. It was not a big check and, as I already mentioned, she had no concept of money. The check came in my name and she never saw one. She had no idea how much we received in her name. She wouldn't have known what any of it meant even if she did. My guess is she thought she was rich.

But she knew she was getting some money each month, and it was her money. One day she asked me about the check. She wanted to know if she could give the money to some kind of Christian ministry, specifically a missionary or an orphan. She said she didn't know which one to give money to, but asked me to look into it. She told me she would trust my judgment to send it to somebody who needed it more than she did. That is what she did with part of her disability check. Looking back at it, I realize that she thought the whole check was going to help somebody else.

I know that some would look at how Elisabeth "served" others and conclude it didn't amount to much. Very few heard her prayers at night when she was alone in her room. There was no fanfare in what she did. She didn't even have a concept of how much or little she was giving to others with her check. Her faith was like the faith of a child. Her giving and service to others, by the world's standards, was so modest.

But I would challenge the reader to look at Christ. When we see Him walking and teaching in the pages of the New Testament, what do you think *He* thought of her servant's heart? We do not have to rely on the biased opinions of a father when we try to answer that question.

Fortunately, the Gospel of Matthew tells us what He thought. To be great in His kingdom, one has to be a servant. The Lord told us what that kind of service might look like. One day, He took a child and placed him in front of His disciples and said:

> Therefore, whoever humbles himself as this little child is the greatest in the kingdom of heaven (Matthew 18:4).

We are so tainted by the world's standards of greatness. Even as Christians we think that great service to the Lord must be on a grand scale. It must involve some grand ministry with a huge budget. But service to others and following the example of the Lord can take place in the humble prayers of a girl with cerebral palsy in a room by herself. It can take place in wanting to give her disability check to somebody she thinks needs it more than she does. In Elisabeth's case, it never occurred to her to let others know she was helping others. I am pretty sure she didn't want us to know she was praying at night for everybody she had ever met. I am also pretty sure she wished she could have given her disability check to others herself, without having to ask her dad to do it.

Being a servant can take place when we use the gifts God has given us, however small the world may consider that service to be. Elisabeth served those who knew her by showing that any believer, even in the midst of hardships, can model the actions of the Suffering Servant. The power of the risen Christ in her made her a servant, just like Him. What a privilege it was to see Him living through and in her.

CHAPTER FIFTEEN

Please, No More Vacation Pictures

Years ago, people used to joke about the friends or distant family members who would invite you to their house after they returned from vacation. They would ask you to come over to eat dinner, play a game, or watch a sporting event on TV. But that was only the lure to get you to come. They would not tell you the real reason.

After dinner, though, you would find out the real reason. In the living room, there was a projector set up with a portable screen. Your host and his family would then show you all the pictures they took on their vacation. You would be subject to at least an hour of the host family laughing and telling the story of each picture—how one of their children got lost at Disneyland, or how another child threw up on one of the amusement rides. There would be pictures of them stopping for gas at the place with the biggest ball of yarn in the world and sitting around the pool at their hotel. Almost everybody my age went through an experience like this.

I even remember sitcoms on television having sketches of this scenario. How do you get out of that situation? You don't want to tell your friends, who just fed you, that you really don't care about their pictures. You didn't go on the trip and you cannot appreciate the humor of each inside joke. You are sure your friend's children are cute, had a good time, and will cherish the memories forever, but their trip means nothing to you and your family. You just can't appreciate how the events of that vacation point to how wonderful your host's kids are.

In the TV episodes, the host family would want to do it more than once, and the invited guests would have to come up with reasons—any excuse at all—as to why they didn't want to come over the next time they were asked. At times like that, it was permissible to lie to get out of such another excruciatingly bad time.

I haven't heard much of situations like that today. Maybe it is because projectors and screens are a thing of the past. Friends and family members send their vacation pictures through their phones or post them on Facebook, and we are free to look at them in the comfort of our own home. We are even free not to look at them at all. We can delete them from our phones. In this case, the things the modern world has brought us are better than the good old days of the past.

There was a fear in writing this book that I would be like the friend who invited the reader over to my house. I have presented the reader with a number of "snapshots" of Elisabeth, and as I mentioned, I can imagine a reader thinking I am just a proud father who is blind to the fact that others do not share my estimation of my daughter. Those outside the immediate family did not see the things I describe. They didn't go on the "vacation" with me.

The reader would be justified in feeling like the invited guest, thinking Elisabeth was not as great as I think she was—saying, in a sense, "Please, no more vacation pictures!"

All of that is understandable, and probably true to some extent. What father does not think everybody should be able to see how great his kid is? We all have a blind spot and cannot fully grasp why others don't want to see our pictures. I am no different. Maybe the only difference is that Elisabeth lived with my wife and me for longer than most children do.

In fact, I may be more prone to blindness than many others. My daughter died young. She lived a life that most would say was tragic. Her life was one that caused others to pity her. But the pictures I show of her are the complete opposite of what the world would say about her. I want those who look at the pictures to see that. I want them to see that she really was as great as I am describing. I have a need for others to recognize these things, even if they weren't there. I want them to see that Elisabeth's life, her example, is something everyone can benefit and learn from. At the same time, I recognize that I am like the obnoxious host who is inviting people to look at my pictures.

In writing about Elisabeth, I have another problem. Ultimately, I am not telling the reader what I think about her. I am telling others what I believe *Jesus* thinks about her. When I show these pictures of her, I am saying that He lived through her and made her more like Him. I am saying that is what made her great.

But how can I know that? As a father, I was blind to her shortcomings. I run the risk of saying she could do no wrong. Perhaps I only saw what I wanted to see. Maybe others saw that she was not as "cute" as I imagined. Maybe in her mind, Elisabeth was able to hide her bitterness toward God and anger toward others, or maybe I just was able to block such things out, only seeing what I wanted to see.

Even more importantly, the Bible itself says that we cannot know all that the Lord will say to any believer when he stands before Him at the Judgment Seat of Christ. In 1 Corinthians 4:5, Paul says as much. We can fool others, and even ourselves, by our actions and words. But only the Lord knows the motives and thoughts of our hearts. Only He knows our character. Every believer will be in the kingdom of God. But every believer must wait until the King comes to evaluate how much we were like Him, how much His Spirit transformed us into what He wanted us to be.

But we are not left totally in the dark about whether our lives, as well as the lives of other believers we know, are pleasing to the Lord. We must remember that when Paul says this in 1 Corinthians 4, he is talking about faithful teachers in the church. He is talking about people who are serving the church and are thus like the Lord, walking like He walked. Paul's point is not that they might be complete frauds, intentionally fooling themselves and those around them. Paul's point is that even those who are faithfully doing what the Lord wants them to do will sometimes have the wrong motives. Every believer still falls short. We are all still sinners. Nobody is perfect.

But that should not keep us from serving the Lord and His people. Paul acknowledges that we all have failings, but we should make it our aim to please the Lord, and through His power, do so. Each day we should desire to become more like Him. When He comes, He will reveal to us what was pleasing to Him and what was not. Don't judge one another when it comes to such things.

The New Testament makes it clear that we can indeed see when believers are maturing in the faith, doing what the Lord calls them to do, and being what He calls them to be. In Acts 6:3, the church picks certain people who are walking by the power of the Spirit of God. Their character was observable to others.

In 1 Timothy 3, Paul says we can definitely notice those in the church who are faithful to the Lord. In Hebrews 13:7 and Philippians 3:17 we are told to follow the example of those who walk by the Spirit and do what the Lord commands. We can look at someone like Elisabeth and say, "The Lord has done a great work in her."

Though I run the risk of being like the man showing pictures of his children, I know that when all is said and done, the Lord will determine if what I saw is true. He will be the One who judges Elisabeth's character and actions. He will say how she served Him in the midst of her difficulties. Still, we are told to take notice of those who live in a way that honors the Lord. As an admittedly biased father, I am simply saying that in many ways, Elisabeth left me with the best example to follow that I have ever seen. I am very confident the Lord will say to her, "Well done!" on that day.

To defend myself, if the reader would allow me, I would point out that those who knew her best would agree with the pictures I have shown of her. One such person was Ellen, her best friend, who knew her for thirty of her thirty-five years. On her Facebook page, on the day my family and I met at the restaurant to remember Elisabeth, Ellen posted the following words:

> A year ago today my lifelong friend Libby left this life. I feel her loss every day. There's no way to express the heartache. I've tried several times to write about what Libby's friendship has meant to me throughout my life,

> but I just can't. My sympathy card to her family still sits on my desk a year later. All I can say is if I spend the rest of my life trying to live up to her love, I'll be so much the better for it. Thank you for making me a better person, my beautiful friend.

Another lifelong friend of Elisabeth is an old army buddy of mine. His daughters grew up with her. When he heard that she had died, he shared his thoughts with our family in a letter. He spoke of knowing her all those years and discussed her role in the world to come and how great she will be. Clearly having seen the fruit of the Spirit in her life, he commented that there was:

> ...no doubt we knew Christian royalty here on earth. We will be able to say in heaven, "She was a friend of mine on earth." Not so much bragging, just a statement. I think she was the sweetest, kindest, most gentle soul I knew.

I suppose such words could be chalked up to people saying kind things to a family that is hurting. But I truly believe it was more than that. Many others had the same reaction. Before she died, and at her funeral, many commented about her character. They used different words. Some spoke about her strong faith in the midst of her difficulties. Some spoke of her joy, perplexed that she always had a smile on her face in the midst of all her problems. Others simply confessed they could not have lived with the same attitude she had.

I am confident that all of these sentiments reflect that people saw Christ in Elisabeth's life. They saw the product of Him living through her. Few of us will go through the difficulties Elisabeth did, but whatever trials we experience, the New Testament teaches us that the Lord can use them to make us more like Him. His Spirit, who lives within every believer, can develop His character in us. Such character will lead to actions that mirror the actions of the Lord. We can have the privilege of being a servant like He was.

As Paul says, none of us will do it perfectly. We will all make mistakes. But if we ask Him to do it, the miracle of the resurrected

Lord living through us will take place. That is not the opinion of a biased father; that is what God's Word tells us.

That is what Elisabeth showed me. I am confident she showed it to others as well.

CHAPTER SIXTEEN

July 14, 2020

As Elisabeth got older, the impact of her disease worsened. At one point, she began to experience pain in her thighs and back. Since she did not bear weight on them, or use them as they were designed to be used, her bones and ligaments did not develop as they should. Her ligaments and certain muscles had contracted. This was a major source of her pain. When she had to move certain parts of her body, such as when she was being dressed, she would often have a sharp experience of that pain.

It was difficult, however, to determine how much pain she was in. She usually did not cry out when it hurt, but only said it was getting worse. When it finally became a daily issue, we took her to many doctors and tried many different solutions. Elisabeth said none of them helped. Eventually, a neurologist suggested we surgically place a pump in her that would automatically administer morphine on a recurring basis.

That never happened. We didn't realize it, but her pain—and evidently her concern that nothing would help—kept her from sleeping. One day, she had what could be called a break from reality. She was awake, but did not communicate and did not realize who any of her family members were. She had a blank stare with a smile on her face, and occasionally she would laugh at something none of us could see.

We weren't sure exactly what was happening and rushed her to the hospital. They admitted her, but the doctors weren't sure either. They thought it was from lack of sleep, but they told us it could also be an infection in her brain. They treated her for the infection and gave her sleep aids.

For three days in the hospital, she did not sleep. Nothing about her condition changed. We began to wonder if she would "return" to us. Eventually, I suppose because of the medicine, she went to sleep. When she woke up ten hours later, she was her normal self. She spoke to us and wondered why we were all in the hospital.

A wonderful neurologist determined a treatment for her pain that did not involve morphine. For the rest of her life, it provided some relief from the pain and allowed her to sleep on a regular schedule. It was a scary time, but we survived that scare.

A few months before she died, we had another frightening episode. As we were getting her up one morning, it was obvious that something was wrong. She was not talking. When we looked at her, she had a little bit of foam around her mouth. Her eyes were closed, and her mouth was shut, clenched tight. We could not open it. We yelled at her, but she did not respond in any way.

I didn't know if she was alive. None of us knew what to do. We thought it might be some kind of seizure, but weren't sure. Pam called 911 and I tried to get her mouth open to make sure she could breathe. The attempts were unsuccessful.

It took fifteen minutes or so for the ambulance to get there. Before it arrived, Elisabeth opened her eyes and mouth. I am not sure how long she was "out." When she came to, she was not her normal self. She could talk but did not recognize any of us. She did not know her name or where she was.

They took her to the emergency room. After some tests and meetings with another neurologist, it was determined that she had indeed had a massive seizure. The doctor told us that as she had gotten older, her brain "shifted" and changed in how she used it. In one of these changes, a part of her brain that was damaged from birth caused this seizure. He said that because of the severity of her cerebral palsy we were fortunate that this was her first such seizure.

A few days later, Elisabeth had another seizure, although not as severe. Fortunately, the doctor caring for her gave her medication that kept her from having any more, at least that we could see. We knew from her twin, Amy, that a person with epilepsy can have small seizures that go unnoticed.

Elisabeth's disease was also affecting her ability to digest food properly. We had been told that as she got older, she would probably need extra help in this area as well, and it was looking like that was going to be the case. I tell you these things not to give you a medical history of Elisabeth, but to give some background to what happened to her.

In the first part of July 2020, our family got hit by some kind of stomach virus. We all got it, including Elisabeth's twin sister, Amy. It caused a little bit of stomach discomfort and indigestion. After it made its way through the rest of the family, Elisabeth got it last.

Like the rest of us, she complained that her stomach was bothering her. She too was having some digestive issues. It had taken the rest of us a day or two to get over it, and we assumed the same would be true for Elisabeth.

But she was having a harder time shaking it. That was not surprising since her cerebral palsy impacted her in different ways. Still, we had decided that if she was not feeling better by the next day, we would take her in to see her doctor. But COVID-19 was prevalent, and doctors were discouraging patients from coming into the office unless it was an emergency. We were reluctant to classify it as an emergency, but agreed we would make the decision the next morning.

The next day was July 14. When we went in to get Elisabeth up, it was obvious that she was not getting better. Her color was a little off, and she was not herself. We were talking with Elisabeth about whether she felt sick enough to go in to see the doctor. She was not as verbal as she usually was, but she said it would be a good idea since her stomach was bothering her.

We moved her from her bed to the chair where she could go to the bathroom. On that chair, we would be able to get her dressed. I was putting her shirt on and looking into her face when suddenly a large amount of liquid oozed out of her nose and mouth—not vomit or food, but a dark, reddish-brown liquid. At the same time, her body immediately went limp.

Pam and Kathryn, our youngest daughter, were in the room with me, helping to get her ready. None of us had any idea what was happening. Because of her cerebral palsy, Elisabeth's body was always stiff. Now, she was slumped over. Even worse, she was completely unresponsive.

A panic came over all three of us. Did this have something to do with her seizures? Was the liquid coming out of her blood? Was she bleeding inside? What were we to do? There was complete chaos in the room. One of us said we ought to call for an ambulance, but we knew from the last experience that it would take around fifteen minutes to get there. If she was bleeding like we thought, we didn't have that much time. We knew we could get to a local emergency room faster, so we bundled her into the car and rushed her to the hospital.

It seems strange how our brains work in a situation like this. As we sped toward the hospital, I was assuring myself that everything would be OK. Elisabeth had survived so much worse. She beat the odds when she was born. She survived her break with reality after a few days in the hospital, and she came through her massive seizure when I thought she had died. I also remembered Amy's brain hemorrhage a few days after the twins were born, when the doctors told us Amy would not survive—which proved to be wrong as well.

We just needed to get her to a doctor. There is no way a stomach virus could be worse than the medical situations we had seen as a family over the years. Half of my brain was reminding me of these things.

But the other side of my brain was telling me it was different this time. When the liquid came out of her nose and mouth as I was dressing her, her beautiful blue eyes instantly changed to grey, and her pupils became very large. Then her eyes closed. The limpness in her body was something none of us had ever seen.

Looking back, I remember hearing that sometimes when people die you can see their life leave in their eyes. Those who say such things point out that God breathed life into us and when that life leaves, sometimes it is obvious. I don't know if that is true or not, but what I saw in Elisabeth's eyes frightened me. As we headed toward the hospital near our home, the same chaos I felt in Elisabeth's room and in the car was happening in my head. One second, I was assuring myself that she was going to be OK. In the next second, I thought about what I had seen a few minutes earlier and knew she was not going to live. In fact, I thought she had already died.

When we arrived at the emergency room, the chaos continued. There was a tent at the entrance of the emergency room to screen people for COVID. We screeched to a halt in front of it. I grabbed Elisabeth and ran through the tent. The nurses tried to stop me, but I yelled I couldn't stop. I kept going past the front desk, back into the restricted treatment area. Neither Elisabeth nor I had a mask on.

As soon as I entered the door, there was a nurse. I grabbed her and told her that my daughter was unresponsive and that she needed to take care of her now. The nurse did so, calling for a doctor nearby to help her.

Pam, our daughter Kathryn, and I then waited in the emergency waiting room. Their minds were doing what mine was. We couldn't believe we were there. But we had been in many hospitals before with both Elisabeth and Amy. We all were hoping this was a repeat. But if we thought they were going to call us back to talk to Elisabeth, reality would soon hit us and tell us that wasn't going to be the case.

After about thirty minutes, they did indeed call us back. In a "family" room, the doctor told us that Elisabeth had died. She was dead when we brought her in. It had taken those thirty minutes for them to heroically try to revive some signs of life in her, and then clean her up so we could see her.

Through a fog, we told him what had happened and asked him what killed our daughter and sister. He said that only an autopsy could tell us for sure, but based upon what he saw, Elisabeth had not been able to digest her food properly for some reason. No doubt, it was because of her cerebral palsy. I suppose the stomach virus may have had something to do with it as well. Some food and liquid had come up and gone into her lungs. When that happened, it caused her heart to stop as well. She died immediately and did not experience pain.

To this day, as with many things doctors have said about Elisabeth's condition through the years, I still don't understand how that works.

But when he told us what had happened, I knew that is what I saw when I last saw Elisabeth's eyes change in her room.

I am sure that part of the doctor's training was to comfort us as much as he could. In that room, he saw that we were completely devastated. I still remember his exact words: "These things happen. There was nothing you could have done. You all did everything you could."

Even in that moment, I thought that in his attempt to be kind to us, he was lying. I thought he was saying those words because there was no benefit in telling the truth. Why should he beat us when we were down, since it was already too late? I was sure he was thinking that I should have taken Elisabeth to the doctor the day before. We should have called the ambulance. We should have done mouth-to-mouth resuscitation and CPR in her room. If we had done any of those things, maybe Elisabeth would still be alive. I assumed he was thinking those things about us because those are the things that went through my brain.

It seems that this "what if" game is common among people who lose loved ones. If only they had done something differently, they would not have seen their family member die. I suppose such feelings will never completely disappear from those who go through such things.

But I try to remember the words of that wise Bible teacher who once told me: "You must give place to the sovereignty of God." It is part of our human make-up to think we can control all aspects of our lives. If we only do our best, we can even determine if our family members live or die. But ultimately, God determines such things. Oftentimes, in His sovereignty, He does things in ways we wouldn't.

The reader would think I would have learned that lesson from the very beginning of Elisabeth's and Amy's lives. From the first day, I was completely powerless to determine if they would live, be able to speak, or even think.

On July 14, 2020, I was not the one in control. I wanted to think I could have saved Elisabeth, and my tendency to beat myself up over my inability to do so is understandable in light of our great loss. We lost our daughter and sister. She was the most pure-hearted, gentle, merciful, loving, peacemaking servant I had ever met. In her, I had the privilege of seeing how Christ could change a person. I saw what He could do through His power while living in her. She had lived in my home for thirty-five years, and on this side of the kingdom of God, she never would again. At times, I might be tempted to think I could have changed that.

My situation can be a learning experience for many. I wanted Elisabeth to stay. But God, in His sovereignty, had other plans.

Because Elisabeth had a hunger and thirst for righteousness, she had told her aunt a few months earlier that she wanted to go home. Her Lord said it was time.

CHAPTER SEVENTEEN

Welcome Home

When Elisabeth and Amy were five years old, our family went on a vacation to Washington, DC. Part of the trip involved a visit to the White House. We contacted the office of our congressional representative in North Carolina and got the required tour tickets. Our congressman even sent us a form letter with the tickets saying we would be his personal guests on the tour. Of course, everybody who went on the tour had the same letter from their own congressman.

At the allotted time, our family joined a group of about fifty other people at the designated place next to the White House. An official tour guide met us and took our tickets. She wore an official uniform and informed us that even though the president and his family actually lived in the White House, it was really *our* home. The president was only temporarily using it. It belonged to the citizens of the United States and for that reason was called "The People's House." Our tickets attested to the fact of who we were. We were some of those citizens. Therefore, the tour guide said, "Welcome home!"

None of us, of course, felt like that was really our home. It was too grand. The tour itself confirmed our thoughts. The rooms, china, and paintings all indicated this place was out of our league. The guide related some of the history that had taken place in those walls, history that had changed the world.

We didn't live in that place. None of us would grab a drink from the refrigerator, sit on a couch, and watch TV. The president, the most powerful man in the world, lived in that home. It was his and his family's home. At that time, it was George Bush, Sr.

About halfway through the tour, we had to go up some stairs. I was pushing Elisabeth in her wheelchair, and she could not go up them. Amy was wearing a brace on her right, shorter, leg. She could walk, but negotiating stairs was very difficult for her. A couple of Secret Service agents approached me and told me to come with them, bringing Elisabeth and Amy along. Pam remained with Emily and Kathryn. The agents didn't tell us why the three of us needed to go with them, but I assumed they would show us an easier way for Elisabeth and Amy to continue the tour. They took us to a small elevator, with a young woman standing there waiting for us.

The young woman and the agents then told us they didn't want to say it out loud in front of the other members of the tour, but they had a surprise for the girls. Not only would Elisabeth and Amy be able to use the elevator to go on the tour, but somebody wanted to meet them. The first lady of the United States, Barbara Bush, was going to come down the elevator and welcome them to the White House. The young woman was her assistant, and the agents were talking on their radios to agents in another part of the White House. Mrs. Bush was on the third floor and would soon be coming down to talk with them.

Elisabeth and Amy were young, but they understood they were about to meet somebody important. They had seen her on television. They knew who the president was. They understood this was quite an honor. I got my camera ready to take pictures of this moment that they would remember all their lives. The assistant and agents were talking with the girls, and the twins were very excited.

I didn't say anything, but I thought maybe the president himself was with his wife. Maybe they both would step off that elevator and talk with the girls. Maybe the agents even knew it but were keeping it a surprise. In any event, we sure would have a story to tell when we joined back up with the group.

We watched the lights on the elevator, waiting for at least Mrs. Bush to arrive. We saw that it stopped one floor above us. We stayed there five or ten minutes as the agents continued to talk on the radio. The elevator eventually came to our floor, but unfortunately, Mrs.

Bush never got off. The agents said an emergency had kept her from coming to see the twins. What a disappointment. We were one floor away!

The girls and I got to continue our tour. I think I was more disappointed than they were when we didn't get to meet the first lady, and maybe even the president. Every time I see the White House, I think about that event. Sometimes I see pictures of dignitaries visiting the White House and having the first lady and president meet them at the front door. Even though it was an honor to visit our "home" in DC, meeting the first lady and president was an honor the girls didn't receive.

Fortunately, there is another, even greater, homecoming that is not like that.

Our Home

The New Testament is full of references that point out that this world is not the home for the believer in Jesus Christ. Our Savior is waiting in heaven, but will one day return to this earth and establish a kingdom that will last forever. Paul says that even now our citizenship is in heaven as we wait for the Lord to return. Our citizenship is there because that is where He is (Philippians 3:20). John says that this present world, our present home, is passing away (1 John 2:17).

Paul says that when a Christian experiences death, he becomes absent from his body but present with the Lord. In fact, Paul says that at the time of death, the Christian is *at home* (2 Corinthians 5:8). We know that the physical bodies of Christians will not be resurrected until the Lord returns. But when a believer dies, his soul goes home to be with the Lord.

We also know that the believer receives some kind of temporary body as he awaits the resurrection. When he is with the Lord he is not just floating around like a ghost. We see an example of this on the Mount of Transfiguration. Moses and Elijah, who had been dead for centuries, appear with the Lord and have a conversation with Him. The disciples on the mountain saw and heard Moses and Elijah.

Our eternal home will be with the Lord on the new earth. This is what the Lord had in mind when He told the disciples that in His Father's *house* there will be *many mansions*. Jesus has gone ahead of us in order to prepare a place for every believer. The result will be that where He is they will be there as well (John 14:1-5).

To put it simply, when a Christian dies, he goes home. Home is where the Lord is. All of this makes sense: those who have believed in Jesus have received eternal life from Him and have become His children. Their home is with Him. Believers who die today go home to be with the Lord in heaven and will return with Him when He comes to earth to establish His kingdom.

A beautiful picture of this is seen at the cross of the Lord. On one side of Him, a thief was dying, as He was dying. This thief believed in Him. As they faced death, the Lord said to Him, "Today, you will be *with Me* in Paradise." Wherever the Lord is, is paradise. For His children, those who are part of His family, that paradise is home.

There is a great example in the New Testament of what it is like for a believer to go home.

Stephen's Homegoing

More than any other book of the Bible, the book of Hebrews speaks about the fact that Jesus is the believer's high priest. Because of Christ, the believer can come before God boldly in prayer, and Christ intercedes for us before the Father. Because of Him, we know the Father hears our prayers. Christ's death on the cross was the one and final sacrifice for sins. After we have believed in Him for eternal life, we have complete access to the throne of God's grace.

That is why the book of Hebrews emphasizes that Jesus is *seated* at the right hand of His Father in heaven. The reason He is seated is because His work is done. There are no more sacrifices to be made. He is now only waiting until He returns to establish His kingdom on earth (Hebrews 1:3,13; 10:12). How appropriate that the eternal King, who has finished His work and is waiting for His kingdom, would be sitting down.

This background is important when we consider the death of the church's first martyr, recorded in Acts 6–7. Stephen was one of the first deacons. He is not pictured as a rich or important man by the world's standards. In fact, he is not even mentioned in the early chapters of Acts or during the earthly ministry of the Lord.

He was chosen for the role of deacon because he was full of the Spirit (Acts 6:3). It was clear to those around him that the Lord was living through him. No doubt they saw the fruit of the Spirit in his life and the character described in the Beatitudes.

But he wasn't chosen simply because his character reflected the Lord. He was chosen because he, like the Lord, was a servant. The need for deacons arose because the church needed servants. Specifically, there were widows in the church in Jerusalem who needed help in their daily allotment of food. It wasn't glamorous work, but Stephen and the other deacons would serve those widows by bringing them food to make sure they did not go hungry.

When Luke continues Stephen's story in the book of Acts, he makes it even clearer that he was like Jesus. Like the Lord, Stephen experienced suffering. He was falsely accused of the same crime Jesus had been accused of (Acts 6:13). Like the Lord, he was put on trial in front of the same court (Acts 6:12) and condemned to die. Even his final words were like the Lord's. Like Jesus on the cross, Stephen committed his spirit to God. Finally, like the Lord, he prayed that God would forgive the sin of those who killed him (Acts 7:59-60).

Luke points out to the readers of Acts that Stephen's martyrdom happened because Stephen was like Christ. The church recognized that he was like Christ as well, and that is why they chose him to be a deacon. The enemies of the Lord hated him because he was like Christ. We can almost hear them say that Stephen was just like their former enemy, Jesus of Nazareth.

When he died, there was a scene of great chaos. His enemies screamed and rushed upon him as a mob to kill him. They stoned him to death. After he died, his fellow believers wept over him (Acts 7:54–8:2).

What a loss for the church in Jerusalem! This man was a servant through whom the Lord was living and working. We are not told his exact age, but he was likely young, with many more years left to be an example to others and serve them. I like to think he was around thirty-five years old, and if so, that was another thing he had in common with the Lord, who was around thirty-five when He was crucified.

Though Stephen's death was a great loss for the church, it was not a loss for Stephen. On that day, Stephen went home to be with the One who had given him life and lived through him.

Immediately before he died, Stephen cried out, "Look! I see the heavens opened and the Son of Man *standing* at the right hand of God!" Many have noticed the contrast here with Jesus in the book of Hebrews. In Hebrews, He is seated. But with the death of this man, He stood up. He was welcoming this faithful servant home. It is a tender picture, but it is more. The Lord was honoring Stephen by rising to meet him. We can only imagine what joy filled Stephen's heart when he saw what he saw in the heavens. He had this joy even though he was going through suffering and a cruel death.

Students of the Bible debate the full significance of what Stephen saw. All believers go to be with the Lord when they die. But do they all get the same welcome that Stephen did? Does the Lord stand and come to meet them? Or does Luke record what Stephen cried out because it was unusual?

I don't know. Perhaps the Lord does stand to meet every single believer when they come into His presence. But this is the only place in the New Testament where we see such a thing. I tend to agree with those who say this was a special honor for Stephen. There were many other believers in Jerusalem during his ministry. But he stood out. He was an example of faithfulness for others to follow. He faithfully endured suffering and honored the Lord by being like Him. The Lord's actions indicate that not only was the Lord welcoming him home, He was welcoming him like a dignitary. Stephen is the kind of believer who will be great in the kingdom of God.

We should rightly look at Stephen as an example of Christ. But we should not fall into the trap of thinking he was the only one like that, and that we cannot possibly be like him. We have a tendency to do that with heroes. The Bible makes it clear there will be many more like him, many more who will be great in the kingdom of the Lord. I am pretty confident I lived with one.

Elisabeth Was Like Stephen

I have come to love the story of Stephen in the book of Acts. Stephen is a hero in the story of the church, and I see so many parallels between him and Elisabeth. There is a decent chance they were roughly the same age. They both lived by the power of the Spirit. The work of the Spirit in their lives was evident to those around them. Neither was important in the eyes of the world.

Both served others in ways that many would call unglamorous, such as providing food to believing widows or praying for others during the night. Even though the sources of their sufferings were different, they both suffered faithfully in the circumstances in which the Lord placed them. They accepted those roles, knowing they were being obedient to the Lord and that the sufferings of this present age were temporary. They both looked forward to going home. Their difficult circumstances contributed to that longing.

Stephen expressed that longing by shouting out what he actually had the privilege of seeing. "Look what I see!" The King of kings, the One whom he served, was personally welcoming him home. In her bedroom on July 14, Elisabeth did not see such a thing, as far as I know. But she did express the same joy as she looked forward to that day. To her aunt, a few months before she died, "I am so ready to go home!" To her mom, "Mom, I sure am going to miss you!" And to me, "Dad, I just cannot wait!"

There was a lot of chaos when Stephen and Elisabeth died. For those who knew them, it was a painful day with a lot of weeping. But what a different scene they both stepped into. The One they loved was waiting for them. Their sufferings would be over in His presence.

Like I said, I don't know if the Lord stands to meet every believer when they go home. Maybe it is like when Elisabeth went to the White House. It was a great tour. The guide welcomed her and told Elisabeth it was her home. Elisabeth was *almost* greeted by the first lady and maybe even the president himself.

It was understandable when that did not happen. The first lady and president are very important and busy people. Something came up. They can't greet everybody. They only have time to do that with dignitaries. Elisabeth certainly wasn't one of those on that day in Washington, DC. The Bush family did not even know her.

But the circumstances were different in her bedroom on July 14. I don't know how the Lord greets every believer who dies. But I am positive that Elisabeth got a greeting fit for a dignitary. It wasn't like waiting for an elevator to come to the first floor, hoping to see somebody important. After all, the King had been living through her for a long time. You could see Him in her. He knew her well. He was at home with her. She talked with Him every night when nobody else was around.

She would get a different greeting this time, and it would be from Somebody even more important than the president of the United States.

In her bedroom, her mom, sister, and I were in panic mode. But at that very instant, she saw her Savior. In whatever temporary body He has given her, she took her first steps. I know He was standing up to meet her when He said, "Welcome home, Elisabeth! Welcome home!"

CHAPTER EIGHTEEN

Greatness in Christ's Kingdom

The twentieth-century Christian author C. S. Lewis is probably best known in the United States for his children's series *The Chronicles of Narnia*. But he also wrote a number of books for adults in which he defended the claims of Christianity using logic.

I once read that when Lewis first began writing and speaking about Christianity, he did not believe there would be differences among Christians in the kingdom of God. Like many, he saw the eternal kingdom as a place of perfect equality.

As time went on, however, he saw that was not the case. There were simply too many passages in the Bible that spoke of rewards for faithfulness and different levels of greatness in the kingdom. It was clear that different believers will receive different rewards. He loved logic, and logic and justice strongly argue for the same conclusion. How just would it be if there were no differences in the kingdom of God between Stephen and a believer who lives a life of ease, fearing what others may think of him? It is impossible to think Stephen would not be rewarded in some special ways.

As a result, Lewis changed his views on this matter. In one of his books, *The Great Divorce,* we can see this change. The book is an allegory, or fable. It records the dream of a man who sees a group of people taking a bus ride to heaven. When they arrive there, they take a tour with a guide. On this tour, they see a number of different people. The people in heaven wear different kinds of robes. There are also different crowns worn by the inhabitants of this heavenly realm.

One encounter stands out. A man on the tour sees a procession coming his way. In the procession are spirit beings throwing flowers, and young boys and girls singing songs whose beautiful melodies outmatched anything heard in any song on earth. They are accompanied by musicians.[2]

Following these spirit beings, singers, and musicians, is a lady. The man observing this scene sees that the procession is clearly being done in her honor. He notices that she stands out because of the "unbearable beauty of her face." Her clothes are different from the clothes of the other people he had seen during his tour of heaven. He wondered: Who could this be?

In his mind, he assumes it is somebody who had been very important on earth. Surely, she was a religious leader or author of some sort. He makes a mental list of famous women and tries to figure out which one this woman was. Lewis records a conversation between the man and the guide:

> "Is it?...is it?" I whispered to my guide.
>
> "Not at all," said he. "It's someone ye'll never have heard of. Her name on earth was Sarah Smith..."
>
> "She seems to be...well, a person of particular importance?"
>
> "Aye. She is one of the great ones. Ye have heard that fame in this country and fame on Earth are two quite different things."

The man then asks the guide about the spirits and the children accompanying her. The guide says the spirits are angels serving her, and the young people following her around are those she had served when she was alive. She had been an example for them to follow and

---

[2] C. S. Lewis, *The Great Divorce* (New York, NY: HarperCollins, 2001). The entire account is found in chapter 12.

a lady who had been merciful to others. All those she had affected in these ways were now rejoicing with her.

Of course, this is a fictitious account. There is no such thing as a bus tour of heaven. Even though we know believers in Christ will be greater than angels in the kingdom, the Bible does not speak of angels following believers around throwing flowers. In this fable, the children are a picture of the joy believers will experience as they are united together in the kingdom. The Bible does not say some believers will be adults and others will be children.

But a fable can present truth, as Lewis does with this lady. In this fictitious account, she is said to be one of the *great ones* in the kingdom. Her dress and appearance set her apart. Those who see her recognize these things. Lewis is pointing out that there will rewards in the kingdom, and some will be greater than others. The Lord repeatedly said the same thing.

Those who will be great in the world to come will often be those who were not great by this world's standards. Even the name Lewis gives this woman when she was on earth, Sarah Smith, could not have been more ordinary. On earth, the man asking the guide the questions would not have noticed her. If he had wondered in this present age who would be great in God's kingdom, the name Sarah Smith would not have made the list.

With this lady, Lewis makes these points clear. A fable can do that even though some of the details do not align with reality. However, if we look at the New Testament in a little more detail, we can get a much more Biblically accurate picture of what being great in the kingdom will really look like.

Rewards in the Kingdom

Most readers of the Bible are aware that there will be crowns given in the world to come. Lewis mentions them in *The Great Divorce*. Related to that is the fact, as we have already seen, that in some of His parables the Lord speaks about some believers ruling over ten cities and others over five cities.

The idea of crowns and ruling over cities points to the different levels of authority believers will have in Christ's kingdom. Those with great authority will be great in the kingdom—like Sarah Smith in *The Great Divorce*.

At its most basic level, having authority in the kingdom—being great in the kingdom—is nothing more than being like Christ Himself. He will have supreme authority. But in His grace, He will delegate authority to others who were like Him.

This sharing in Christ's rule, this sharing in His authority, implies that those who are given this privilege will be closer to Him in His kingdom. They will share a greater intimacy with Him.

There is much we do not understand about these rewards and what they will mean to those who receive them. The New Testament describes many different kinds of rewards, not just crowns and ruling over cities. Two specific rewards may help us understand what it will look like: a new name and a seat of honor.

A New Name

Nicknames are common in families, especially between spouses. Often, they are private names that nobody else uses. It may be, in this most intimate relationship of marriage, that the spouses only use these special names when nobody else is around. Others may not even know the nickname exists. This practice of special names is often carried over to children and even close personal friends. This is true even for famous people. For example, only close friends and family members called Martin Luther King, Jr. "Mike." Special names indicate an intimacy among those who use them.

We see this practice used in the Bible. The real name of the man we call *Peter* in the Bible was *Simon*. When he meets the Lord for the first time, the Lord says he will be called *Peter* (John 1:42). This new nickname means "rock." The Lord evidently gave him this special name because He knew that in the future Peter would be a leader among the disciples. He would eventually be the rock the others could look up to, a rock they would eventually be able to lean on.

It was not a coincidence that Jesus gave a nickname to Peter. He was, after all, one member of the inner circle of disciples who was closest to the Lord.

Jesus also gave nicknames to two other disciples in His inner circle. He called James and John the "sons of thunder" (Mark 3:17). Some say this nickname is a negative one, given to them because they were hot-tempered, but there is probably a better explanation for it.

These two men were fervent followers of the Lord. Perhaps they were bold speakers when Jesus sent them out to proclaim the good news. This explanation fits their history. Of the original group of twelve disciples, James became the first to be martyred for his faith. No doubt this happened to him because he fearlessly preached Christ in a nation that had executed Him.

James' brother, John, faithfully proclaimed Christ in the midst of much suffering for around sixty years after becoming a disciple of Christ. He was even exiled to a deserted island for spreading the teachings of Christ. Both of these brothers were "spark plugs," that is, sons of thunder, for the Lord.

I think it is safe to say that Peter, James, and John treasured the fact that the Lord had a nickname for each one of them. One can imagine Simon telling a friend that the Lord Himself referred to him as a "rock" and that is why he preferred the name *Peter* over *Simon*. When John looked back on his life and saw how he had been slow to learn the things the Lord taught him, he must have been thrilled when he thought about what Jesus called him. From the very beginning, Christ had recognized that, like thunder from the sky, John would loudly and boldly proclaim the teachings of the Lord to others. He liked being known as a son of thunder.

In the last book of the New Testament, the Lord sends a letter to a church in a place called Pergamum. The church was going through hard times, with at least one of its members being martyred. Jesus encourages the believers in Pergamum to remain faithful to His name, for those who do so will receive various rewards in the kingdom—including a "new name" which nobody knows except the Lord and the one who receives it (Revelation 2:17). A similar promise is given to the church in Philadelphia in Revelation 3:12. Simply put, Jesus says the believer who is faithful to *His name* during difficult times will receive a new name.

What will receiving a special name from the Lord mean in His kingdom? We are not told exactly. Some have suggested the person will be invited to certain events as the honored guest of the Lord. Whatever it will mean, it is clear that this kind of nickname will indicate a closer relationship with the King. Even on earth that was the case. The Lord had many disciples during His ministry who were believers and will be in His kingdom, but the New Testament tells us that some were closer than others. Peter, James, and John were the closest three disciples the Lord had. As we have seen, each of them was given a new name from Him.

When we speak of who will be greatest in the coming kingdom, it stands to reason that it will be those who are closest to the Lord. He will share His rule especially with those who were like Him, and for all eternity He will call them by names that have special significance. Only they and their Lord will use those names in their interactions with Him. It will be like special names between the closest people on earth, like a husband and wife.

Not surprisingly, those with these new names will have another reward: a seat of honor.

A Seat of Honor

In the United States, those who are elected as our leaders are said to have won a "seat" in Congress. The head of the House of Representatives sits in the "seat" of the Speaker of the House. Perhaps the clearest image of the president's power is when we see him sitting at the presidential desk in the Oval Office. A king sits upon a throne, which is the most obvious symbol of the ruler's authority in his kingdom. From the throne, the king hands down his decisions.

The New Testament tells us Jesus will sit upon His throne when He returns and sets up His kingdom. It will be a throne of "glory," which indicates power. In His case, it will signify ultimate authority (Matthew 24:31). When the angel told Mary that she would give birth to this coming King, he told her that He will sit upon this throne forever (Luke 1:32-33).

Just as in other kingdoms, the Lord will not rule by Himself. In His grace, He will share His rule and authority with others. There will be other seats of authority. For example, He told the disciples that they themselves would sit upon twelve thrones when He sat on His. On those thrones, they too would exercise the privileges of those in power (Matthew 19:28).

The disciples understood that the Lord would reward some with authority in His kingdom, and this authority would involve where one would be able to sit. Two of them asked Jesus if He would let them "sit" upon His left and His right when that day came (Mark 10:37). This was a bold request! We use the phrase "the boss's right-hand man" to refer to the second most powerful person in an organization. These disciples were asking to be the two men with the most authority in the eternal kingdom of God, outside of the Lord Himself. Jesus' throne would be in the middle, while their thrones would be on each side of His. They pictured the three of them sitting together in this manner.

The Lord did not rebuke them for thinking such seats of power will exist. In fact, He said these seats of authority will indeed be given when He comes to rule (Mark 10:35-45). The problem these two disciples had was that they did not realize who would sit on these thrones. These positions will be given to those who were servants like the Lord, not to those who thought they could obtain these positions because they knew Jesus, or because they asked for them before anybody else thought to ask. These two positions will be given to those who were most like the servant King.

Jesus will indeed have a right-hand and a left-hand man in His kingdom. But there will be other seats of honor as well. In His letter to the believers at the church in Laodicea, He said the one who serves Him will sit down with Him on His throne (Revelation 3:21). His throne will symbolize authority in His kingdom, but He will share that authority with *all* who were like Him. Not all faithful disciples will sit on His left or right. There will only be two such positions. But there will be many other believers who will rule with Christ. All faithful disciples will share, in different degrees, in that rule, and in that sense, they too will sit on His throne.

But seats of honor do not occur only in government. People are also honored by where they sit on special occasions, such as at a wedding or an important celebration dinner. We often use the phrase "the head table" to describe such situations.

When I was in the military, I attended many official dinners. Many of them were what we call *gala events*. There was always a head table, where the honored guests would sit with the commander. In such an environment, the commander always had his right-hand and left-hand men who would sit with him as well. A person's authority and power determined at which table he or she would sit. The more power people had, the closer they sat to the head table.

Likewise, at a wedding reception dinner celebrating the union of a couple as man and wife, there is a head table where those who are closest to the couple sit. The closer a person is to the bride or groom, the closer to that table he or she will sit.

In one of His parables, the Lord spoke about this custom. He told His disciples that when they are invited to a dinner they should sit in the lowest seat. That would allow the person hosting the dinner to come and invite them to move up to a higher seat, a seat with more honor (Luke 14:7-11).

The Bible teaches us that when the Lord returns to set up His kingdom, a dinner like that will take place. In Revelation, John refers to it as the marriage supper of the Lamb (Revelation 19:9). Jesus is the groom and the church is the bride. Jesus described the beginning of His kingdom as a great feast put on by a king (Luke 14:15-24) and told the disciples He would finish the Lord's Supper with them when He returned (Matthew 26:29). Yes, there will be eating in the kingdom of God!

This particular feast will celebrate the fact that Christ has returned and His kingdom has begun. It will be the most gala dinner of all time.

At that dinner, then, there will be seats of honor. Certainly, the ones who will sit on Christ's right and left hands will be at whatever the "head table" is. The Lord referred to this event in His encounter with the centurion, whom He called a man with *great* faith. He commented that people like that man would sit at a table of honor with other men of great faith, such as Abraham, Isaac, and Jacob (Matthew 8:10-11). Imagine sitting at that table!

The author of Hebrews quotes from Psalm 45 when he writes about the coming of the King. Psalm 45 is a psalm about a royal wedding celebration, where the King will have those who are particularly close to Him. They are called His "companions" (Hebrews 1:9), or intimate partners. The New Testament makes it clear that these companions are believers who were like Him. They will be given seats of honor at the marriage supper of the King.

All believers will be at this feast. All believers will be full of joy as they celebrate the beginning of the kingdom of God. But some will be closer to the Lord than others. They will be sitting closer to Him, and He will have a new name for each one of them. While none of us can completely understand what that will look like, I think we can see a better picture of it than Lewis did in the allegory *The Great Divorce.*

CHAPTER NINETEEN

Who Is That Regal Woman Sitting There?

Before the coming of the kingdom, the bodies of all believers will be resurrected from their graves. They will be in glorified bodies, not subject to sin, disease, or death (1 Corinthians 15:35-50). These are the bodies believers will possess forever. They will replace the temporary form of existence that believers have now when they die and enter the presence of the Lord.

After this resurrection, believers will appear before the Judgment Seat of Christ. Here, the Lord will reward them for what they had done during their earthly lives. It is here that the various crowns will be given. It is here that new names will be given to those who honored the name of the Lord. It is here that seats of authority in the kingdom will be handed out by the One who has all authority. In their resurrected, glorified bodies, believers will take part in the coming feast that will mark the beginning of eternity.

Just as the guests at an official military dinner wear their uniforms, displaying their military awards and insignia of rank, believers at the marriage supper of the Lamb—which will occur after the Judgment Seat of Christ—will be able to see one another's rewards that each received from the Lord. Whatever rewards, such as crowns, the Lord has given to each believer will be evident to all, even if at this time we do not understand how they will look.

It is simply impossible for us to even come close to realizing what that will be like. To begin with, time will be different for us on that day. How long will this celebration take? A week? A month? There will be so much to share with all those in attendance. Imagine the things that will be said!

Imagine, also, what it will be like for those who will be great in the kingdom of God. These are the ones who faithfully endured suffering for Christ. Stephen was found guilty in an earthly court and condemned to death. Before the court of the Lord, he will be greatly rewarded. In the book of Acts, the last picture we see of him is him lying on the ground dead, having been rejected by the leaders of his nation. On that future day, he will be given a seat of honor by the eternal King.

A similar thing is true for the man born blind in John 9. He too was treated with contempt by a human court. He was expelled from the synagogue. He had suffered his whole life. If his actions on the day the Lord healed him are any indication, he too will be highly exalted when he stands before the Lord.

Both of these men were considered insignificant by the people of their day. In the case of the man born blind, the Lord said he suffered like that not because his parents had sinned, but in order that the works of God might be displayed in him (John 9:3). These works certainly included the fact that Christ healed him—nobody had ever cured a man born blind. But there are other ways in which the works of God would be displayed in him. In Christ, he received eternal life. In Christ, his body will rise from the dead.

Still, the works of God include even more than these incredible realities. In Christ, this man will rule and have great authority in an eternal kingdom. Think about the power of God accomplishing that. A man who had begged his whole life. A man who was despised by those in power on earth. A man whose neighbors saw him as cursed by God. A man like that, exalted and given an eternal throne, a seat of high honor. That would be quite the display of the greatness of the power and grace of God. Who, in their wildest dreams, could imagine a future for somebody like that when they saw him begging in the streets of

Jerusalem? In other words, the power of the Lord is most clearly seen when He exalts the weak. And what an exaltation that will be!

The same, of course, was true for Stephen. A man who served widows their food and was left lying in a pool of blood was not seen as a great man in his day. But the power of Christ will result in him being a man of greatness in that future eternal kingdom. He was so great in Christ's eyes that He rose from His seat at the right hand of His Father to meet him.

I am convinced the same can be said for Elisabeth. Who, during her life, could fathom her being a great queen in Christ's eternal reign? She could not even walk on her own power. As in the case of the man born blind, only the power of Christ could bring about such an exaltation, and such a change in status.

In my life's experiences, the closest illustration I have seen of something like this is from my time in the military. When the Medal of Honor recipients receive their medal for their actions, they and their families are the special guests of the president at the White House, even spending the night there. For the rest of their lives, they receive extra money from the government. They receive a unique medal that they wear around their necks, even in civilian clothes. When they travel, they are given special consideration. Their children can attend any military academy, such as West Point, without going through the stringent admissions process like everybody else does. They are invited to be the guests of honor at numerous parades and dinners. In each case, they are given the seat of honor. They are also given a new name. They will always be called "Medal of Honor Recipient."

Christ will have His Medal of Honor recipients in His kingdom. There will be seats of honor for them.

I am not sure, exactly, how it will be on that day. None of us are. But based upon what the New Testament teaches us, I think it will be close to how I see it in my mind. When the Lord returns and the celebration begins, every believer will be a part of the joyous events. The authority one will have in Christ's rule will determine how close he will be sitting to the King.

I am not so biased to think that Elisabeth will be sitting on His left or right hand. The history of Christ's church is a long one, and there have been many men and women who have served others and endured hardships and persecutions for Him. The Lord will determine how great each believer will be in His Kingdom. But whatever seat Elisabeth occupies on that day, I have no doubt she will be sitting closer to the Lord than I will be. There will be other believers around me. Eventually, one will see Elisabeth and ask the same question the man asked his tour guide in Lewis' fable.

Who is *that* lady? The question will concern the lady who is sitting so close to the Lord. She will be sitting at one of the tables in the kingdom set apart for the King's Medal of Honor recipients. There will not even be a hint of the ravages cerebral palsy had inflicted upon her during her previous life. Like the woman in Lewis' story, someone will comment on the "unbearable beauty of her face." By her location, by her dress, and by whatever other indications there are, it will be obvious that she is royalty. She is one of the great ones.

I have often wondered how well we will know each other at the beginning of the kingdom. I have often been asked that question by others. I am not sure. We will certainly know the believers we knew on earth, and I know we will get to know other believers as we meet them in the kingdom. We will get to know, for example, the people we have read about in the Bible. But it will take time. We won't automatically know everyone there as soon as the kingdom begins. But we will have plenty of time to get to know them!

Somebody around me will know who she is. Maybe they knew her during her earthly life. Maybe they met her before she stood at the Judgment Seat. In any event, they will say that her name is Elisabeth. It will be said that Elisabeth is a fitting name for such a regal woman. That was the name of the mother of John the Baptist, the greatest prophet who ever lived before the coming of Christ. Luke tells us that she was chosen for this honor because the way she lived was pleasing to the Lord (Luke 1:5-6). I can picture somebody at the table commenting that Elisabeth was an elegant name. Maybe someone will point out that in the King James Version of the New Testament it was spelled with an "s".

I suppose that, as in the case of all those sitting close to the Lord, people will wonder what the Lord calls her. What special name did He give Elisabeth? Whether that is discussed or not, none of us will know that name.

I look forward to that day. I already know what I am going to say, however all the details play out. I will comment that, like the rest of them, I don't know what the Lord will call her for the rest of eternity. We will all simply know that it will be a fitting nickname, just like with Peter and the sons of thunder

Then, I will tell them that all of them will call her Elisabeth. But I am still going to call her Libby.

Elisabeth, a year before she went home. She is wearing her treasured Romans 8:18 necklace.

CHAPTER TWENTY

A Sister's Tribute

When I think back on Elisabeth's life, and how I saw Christ in her, I realize she displayed Christ in many ways that were easy not to notice. Her sister Kathryn reminded me of one of those ways. To understand, the reader needs a little background information.

When Elisabeth used an electric wheelchair, since she did not have good use of her hands, she would often accidently hit people with her chair. The chair would lunge forward or backward without any warning for those standing around. Sometimes that would involve running over a family member's foot. Other times, the parts of the chair that supported her legs would hit our shins. The chair was very heavy, and such events caused sharp pain. Elisabeth would often have a tray on her chair, and that tray was able to strike those around her in parts of the body higher than the legs, especially if you were leaning over. The same was true even when we were pushing her in her manual chair. The one doing the pushing might not see others around and accidently hit them. If you spent a lot of time around Elisabeth, there would be evidence of her presence on your body.

Elisabeth, however, had more marks on her than any of us. Many places are not built for large wheelchairs, and if she was navigating around a corner, she would often hit one of her feet on the wall. The same thing was true if we were pushing her in a manual chair.

There were also other kinds of accidents. If she was using a manual chair, in some vehicles she would not be as securely fastened as we would have liked. We could secure the chair, but her straps around her chest in those chairs were not as sturdy and might slip if there was a very sharp turn or a very sudden stop. Occasionally, because she did not have core strength in her body, this would happen and she would slip out of her chair and fall to the floor of the car. Those sitting around her would stick out their arms to try and break her fall. But these falls would leave a mark on her as well.

One of the amazing things about Elisabeth is how good-natured she was about all of these things. While lying on the floor of whatever vehicle she was in, she would always laugh. It seems pretty obvious that she developed a high tolerance for pain.

After Elisabeth died, Kathryn wrote her thoughts on these experiences with her older sister. Even in these everyday events, Kathryn's words show in another way how we saw Christ in Elisabeth:

Bruises

Bruises are my family crest.
An unspoken badge we all bore on our chests
Legs
Arms
And necks

Between the wheels
And the trays
And the narrow hallways
No one saw but us

Bruises, were a must

When I was ten
On one of a million moves
In a crammed hotel room
I placed her tray on her chair like a million times
before...

But the control stick got hit
and it crushed me into the wall

My shins that fall
Looked like hers for once

If there was a log
Of all the times she hit her toes
We could line it back-to-back
And circle the globe

Once, on the way home
As we rounded a sharp curve
She fell out of her chair

Pretzeled, and pinned
And her face in the dirt
She giggled all the way home
Her foot was black for weeks.

These...
are my memories

That I bump into
That leave me black and blue
The tender reminders of her impact

The evidence of a colossal crash
That once...we made contact

On the day she died
On my left thigh
As my dad and I
Lifted her into the van
I got my last bruise because of that chair...
And so did she.

When I began to write this piece
it was about her.

But as her life always did...
her death likewise pointed to Him

For bruises are my family crest...
He bore them on His hands
Arms
And chest...

And although I cannot see...
I know she stands beside nail pierced feet

CHAPTER TWENTY-ONE

Conclusion

In his physical trials, Paul learned that God's grace was sufficient for him. When Elisabeth's twin, Amy, appeared to be dying, I got to experience it as well. But the clearest example of the sufficiency of God's grace that I have personally witnessed was the thirty-five years of Elisabeth's life.

In Amy's case, we understood the magnitude of God's grace when we could rest in the promise of eternal life at the darkest time of our lives. But in Elisabeth, I was taught that God's grace can carry us through so much more.

God extends His grace to us during hardships of various kinds. It is a grace that allows the sufferer to rejoice in the trials he is experiencing because he rests in God's promise that He is using those difficulties to make him more like Christ. What greater privilege could a person have than to experience Christ living through him? Just as Jesus suffered while on earth, He can live through the sufferings of a woman with cerebral palsy like Elisabeth. He can live in and through us as well.

To the degree that the believer is like Christ, he will be great in Christ's kingdom. The obedient believer can believe that as Christ is transforming him through his sufferings, He is preparing that believer for a glorious role for all eternity. Elisabeth had that kind of faith.

G. H. Lang, a Christian writer of the twentieth century, commented about the extreme suffering many Christians experience. He said that in these things, God is "giving to these future rulers the severe training which is indispensable to fitting them for such responsible duties and high dignities."[3]

It is not surprising that Elisabeth's favorite Bible verse was Romans 8:18. Her mom had a special necklace made with the words inscribed on it. She never took that necklace off. After talking about how faithful believers who suffer with Christ will reign with Him, Paul writes:

> For I consider that the sufferings of this present time are not worthy *to be compared* with the glory which shall be revealed in us (emphasis added).

There is a glorious kingdom coming. The King of glory will rule over it. But He will share that glory with believers to the degree that they are faithful in suffering with Him. Elisabeth humbly accepted her physical condition, believing what her Savior told her. She believed in His goodness even though He allowed her to live in the body she had. She served Him in the ways she could because He promised her that He would reward her for doing so. He told her that her reward—the glory He would give her—would far outweigh her afflictions in this life. As great as her troubles were, and as hard as it is to believe, Paul says it is ridiculous to even compare those troubles with the rewards Christ will give her!

That is the marvelous grace of the Lord.

That is the subject of this book. That is why it was written. Elisabeth left an example of what the grace and power of Christ can do in a person's life.

For the unbeliever, that grace offers eternal life as a free gift by faith alone in the promise Jesus gave. All who believe in Him for eternal life will receive it and will live with Him forever.

For the one who has already believed, His grace extends even further. He offers the power of His resurrected life living through us. If we rely on that power, He will miraculously change us into one who is more and more like Christ. The believer needs to ask the Lord to

---

[3] G. H. Lang, *The Epistle to the Hebrews: A Practical Treatise for Plain and Serious Readers* (London, EN: The Paternoster Press, 1951), 52-53.

change him in this way through the Holy Spirit who lives within him. At night, Elisabeth often prayed that prayer. He clearly answered it.

All of us will experience difficulties in this life. They come in many different forms. The list is practically endless. The vast majority of us will not have to go through the persecutions of Paul or Stephen, or endure the sufferings involved with cerebral palsy. But all of us will go through other kinds of hardships. These may include other illnesses, the death of loved ones, financial difficulties, spouses who abandon the family, or the loss of acquaintances because of one's Christian faith.

These difficulties, in whatever form they come, are a major part of the process through which Christ can transform His children. They teach us to rely on Him and on His grace. When He strengthens the suffering believer in this way, that believer experiences an intimacy with Him through the help He provides. The suffering believer also has the privilege of knowing he is walking in the footsteps of the Man of Sorrows. Finally, the believer who is faithful through these hardships will see the character of the King formed in him. That believer will experience the miracle of the resurrected Lord living through him. And such a life will result in hearing the King say "Well done!" when He comes.

How comforting it is to know that this power and these blessings are not only offered to the rich and powerful. In fact, it is often those who are weak and poor, the *Sarah Smiths* of the world, who most often experience them. In Christ's kingdom, I am convinced that most of His "Medal of Honor" recipients will come from that group. Elisabeth showed that to me. Perhaps she can be an encouragement for some who read this book for the same reason.

That is the kind of Savior Jesus is. He gives eternal life as a free gift. He offers the joy of having Him live through us—intimacy with Him—in this life. He gives glorious eternal rewards for faithfulness. In Him, even the most difficult trials of this life can result in the good of His children. The gifts that flow from Him defy imagination. In this book, I have tried to describe what these things mean for somebody like Elisabeth. It was a feeble attempt. I know the reality will be even greater than I can conceive.

Jesus is a generous giver! As the infinite God and the eternal King, it would be impossible for it to be any other way. The wonderful news is that the rewards He offers are available to all His children. They are not just for the healthy, strong, wise, and those we see as important in this world. In fact, most of the time it is just the opposite.

Have you noticed that in the Bible, those who catch the attention of the Lord, those who are commended by Him, are most often those the world considers unimportant? We have already seen that to be the case with a man born blind, who was relegated to begging to even survive. The same was true concerning a poor woman, hemorrhaging blood and despised by her neighbors. Stephen was another example. Even the original disciples of the Lord, those who would become His closest friends, were despised by the rich and powerful of the day. These men would all suffer greatly because of their association with Him.

But there are so many more. Those who study the book of Mark point out that one of the central figures is a man by the name of Bartimaeus (Mark 10:46-52). Of all the people Jesus heals in the book, Bartimaeus is the only one who is named. Like the man born blind, Bartimaeus is poor and an outcast, a man whose life is full of difficulties.

These trials, however, have helped make him a man that relies on the mercy of God. When he hears that Jesus is near him, he repeatedly cries out for that mercy. He knows Christ can heal him.

Others in the book of Mark have believed that Jesus is the Christ. So does Bartimaeus. But he is unique among those believers. He is the only one in Mark that calls Jesus by a particular title. He shouts out that Jesus is the "Son of David." This was a title of great dignity and power. David was the greatest king in the Old Testament and the Messiah would be a descendant of David. Bartimaeus recognizes the majesty of Jesus of Nazareth in a way that is not declared by anybody else in the Gospel of Mark. This is a profound statement by Bartimaeus. Jesus is on His way to Jerusalem to die on a cross when this blind man shouts out that He is the mighty Son of David.

When Bartimaeus calls out to the Lord, the crowds tell him to be quiet. Surely, they thought, Jesus did not want to be bothered by someone unimportant like him.

But this blind man does not escape the notice of the Lord, even though there was a large crowd of people wanting to be around Him and seeking His attention. The Lord singles him out. He calls for him to come to Him. Bartimaeus jumps up with joy to go into His presence. After the Lord heals him, he follows Him to Jerusalem.

This is a literary device—a picture. Bartimaeus is one who recognizes the majesty of Jesus. He is willing to walk on the same road He is traveling, even though it is a path that involves intense suffering. Mark wants his readers to look at Bartimaeus and see that he is a man the reader of Mark can emulate.

The same could be said for another "unimportant" person in Mark's Gospel. Jesus is in the temple one day, with thousands of people walking around. But only one catches His eye. It is a poor lonely widow (Mark 12:41-44). Nobody else notices her, not even the disciples. But Jesus says that of all the people in the temple that day, this woman, with her troubles as a constant companion, is more pleasing to God than anybody else in the crowds. This would include the rich, who had given large sums of money.

Her humility is striking, and, as with Bartimaeus, her afflictions played a large role in producing that characteristic in her. When she gave her small offering, how completely insignificant it would have seemed, even if anybody had noticed her. No doubt, she felt the same way. We can picture her trying to disappear in the crowd, almost ashamed that her two small coins were all she had to give to the Lord. But she served Him with what she had. As a humble servant, she too is an example for all who see her.

I must admit that I never read about the widow in the temple that day without thinking of Elisabeth and her disability check. She didn't want anybody to know, she just wanted to give it to somebody else because that is what she thought the Lord wanted her to do.

There are believers the world does not notice. Often times, even the church does not. People like Elisabeth. It is true that Christ loves the whole world (John 3:16). He gives eternal life to every believer as a free gift by faith alone. He rejects none (John 6:37).

But there are people the Lord has His eyes on in a particular way (John 14:21, 23). He sees them in the crowds, when others don't even recognize they are there. Almost always, like Him, they are acquainted with difficulties. But they are also those who magnify His grace and power, because He is also in the business of making such children of His great in His kingdom.

The good news is that every believing reader of this book can be just like them.

It is no wonder that others have found these things to be true as well. Some have even put such truths into song. Annie Flint was such a believer. After being orphaned at a very young age, and then suffering intense pain for most of her life as the result of various physical ailments, she wrote a hymn about the grace and goodness of Christ that she experienced in her difficulties:

> He giveth more grace when the burdens grow greater,
> He sendeth more strength when the labors increase;
> To added afflictions He addeth His mercy,
> To multiplied trials, His multiplied peace.
>
> His love has no limits, His grace has no measure,
> His power has no boundary known unto men;
> For out of His infinite riches in Jesus
> He giveth, and giveth, and giveth again.[4]

Elisabeth's favorite chorus was from another song that speaks of difficulties. But the focus in the refrain was not on her troubles, but on the One who had made so many wonderful promises to her. Because of Him, she knew her sufferings were temporary and would one day be forgotten. In fact, they could be used in her life in a way that would result in great rewards when this world has passed away. I wish every reader could have heard how loudly she sang this chorus every chance she had the opportunity to do so. I still can hear her sing the words:

---

[4] "He Giveth More Grace," by Annie Flint.

Turn your eyes upon Jesus,
look full in His wonderful face,
and the things of earth will grow strangely dim,
in the light of His glory and grace.[5]

---

5 "Turn Your Eyes Upon Jesus," by Helen H. Lemmel.

Made in USA - Kendallville, IN
64986_9781943399482
03.09.2023 1319